Lili

Lili

Lili Stern-Pohlmann in conversation with
Anna Blasiak

Holland House

www.hhousebooks.com

Paperback ISBN: 978-1-910688-60-1
Hardback ISBN: 978-1-910688-51-9

Cover design by Ken Dawson, Creative Covers

Typeset by Polgarus Studio

Published in the UK

Holland House Books
Holland House
47 Greenham Road
Newbury, Berkshire RG14 7HY
United Kingdom

www.hhousebooks.com

This book is for Karen, my beloved daughter and grandchildren Corey, Daniel and Kaelin, and my little great-grandson Asher, whom I am yet to meet... May theirs be a world of Love and Peace, devoid of hatred & prejudices...

It is in blessed memory of my dearest Mother, who died in London in 2001, and for all my Loved Ones who perished in the Holocaust in 1942/3. They live in our hearts and are remembered daily.

I wish to pay special homage to those Extraordinary Ordinary People, who, in history's darkest hour, "extended a hand" and whose courage and humanity helped save lives of the oppressed.

Lili

Engagement photo of Lili's parents Cecylia Brück and Filip Stern, 1929

CONTENTS

EDITOR'S FOREWORD

By Robert Peett

After Holland House Books had published a novel about the Katyń Massacre, Magda Raczyńska of the Polish Cultural Institute introduced me to the poet and translator Anna Blasiak, who was hoping to publish a series of interviews with a remarkable Holocaust survivor: Lili Pohlmann. We met, and Anna outlined that story, which did indeed sound unusual and significant. As Philippe Sands says in his introduction, each story is unique and casts new light on what might seem known and tired; history becomes forgotten or distorted, or concealed, and the voices of survivors need to be heard. Without Anna Blasiak this story would not have come to light and would not be published or read by you.

I asked Anna why this was all of such interest to her, and she explained that growing up in Poland she had heard little if any of what happened to the Jews, particularly in Poland. All nations have their myths, and stories that conflict with them are too often overlooked, to the detriment of the health of the nation, and for Anna discovering these stories has become a lifelong interest. I suggested that we needed to hear Anna's voice in the book, for her to be a guide, showing just why such a story as Lili's matters now to her, to Poland, and to the rest of the world. Anna's beautiful and moving introductions to each chapter, along with the sharp historical contexts provided by the historian and biographer

Clare Mulley, give an immediacy and perspective to the account of Lili's early life as she tells Anna her story.

Ultimately, this book is about Lili, and specifically about that period of her life when she lost family and childhood, and found unexpected compassion and bravery; when she learnt about evil and yet found goodness; when, in the midst of so much loss and horror, she found a belief in humanity that has continued to this day. Here her story is essentially about her experiences during and just after the Second World War; yet since then she has lived a rich, passionate and happy life, during which she has given so much love and hope to others, as the pieces here by Philippe and Aleksander Skotnicki testify: and especially she has given love and hope to the children in the schools she has visited and continues to visit, helping them know the past and see a better future.

INTRODUCTION

By

Philippe Sands

I first came across Lili Pohlmann back in the spring of 2016. The name was passed on by a colleague in my barrister's chambers who had taken a telephone call from, as she put it, "a delightful and very polite lady." "She has seen a film you were involved in on the BBC, and would like to speak to you about it," my colleague explained. "She said she has a lot more to contribute, she was a child in Lvov during the war, and she found your programme very moving."

A few days later we spoke. Lili introduced me to her story, to the material that is the subject of this fine book. In the course of the conversation she spoke with warmth and sadness, about her memories and sense of identity, of the feelings of connection with the extraordinary city – Lwów, Lvov, Lemberg – that was her home. It was a joy to be in touch with her, back then and again over time.

It is an even greater joy – although tinged with a deep sadness at some of the memories she recounts – to be able to read an account that is more full and detailed, the colours even more vivid. I read the pages of the war years with a special attention, as she described the city and environs of my own grandfather's family. The details she recounts – the initial Soviet years, including the arrival of the Bolshoi ballet with their revolving stage, followed by the arrival of the

1

Germans in the summer of 1941 – is known to me, in broad strokes and in points of detail.

Yet, every story is unique, and special, and important, and must be told. Lili brings those times back to life, allows us to understand that those who were caught up – including those who were lost, like her beloved father and brother, in a time of unique and savage brutality, during the 'agonising days' after Hans Frank, the lawyer and the Governor General of German occupied Poland from October 1939, arrived in the city in August 1942 – were individuals. Each had hopes and loves and anxieties and foibles. Together they were a group, amongst those that caused Rafael Lemkin and Hersch Lauterpacht to offer to the world their ideas on 'genocide' and 'crimes against humanity'.

Yet, we recall too that it is not all darkness and sadness. 'There is a crack in everything, that's how the light gets in', the poet Leonard Cohen once wrote and sang. Indeed. Into Lili's life sprang the remarkable Irmgard Wieth, a German lady who hid Lili and her mother in her apartment for a year and saved their lives, even as she came face to face with the genocidaire that was Fritz Katzmann.

It is our privilege that Lili survived. It is our fortune that she has been able to recall, that she has gathered her memories, that she feels able to talk about them, and that she has now committed her experiences to the page. That she has done this with such acuity, and with a deep sense of humanity, adds to the resonance of her experience.

It is a privilege to read you, dear Lili Pohlmann, dear child of Lwów, so generously and elegantly assisted by Anna

Blasiak. May your words inspire us, remind us, invigorate us, and cause us to redouble our efforts to root out such terrors wherever they are at risk of occurring again.

London & Bonnieux
July 2020

CHAPTER ONE
CHILDHOOD
29 March 1930 – 31 August 1939

*

Anna Blasiak: July 2019, I'm on the train, heading to London to meet Lili Pohlmann née Stern. The train takes me along the Kent coast where I now live afters years in London, then further away from the sea. The green landscape shimmers and sways in the hot sun. I watch it closely from the inside of the air-conditioned carriage. The closer I get to London, the less and less colour there is, everything looks paler, more washed out.

I think about Lili's train journeys all those decades ago – about travelling from Kraków to Lwów every year to spend Passover with her grandparents, about the more traumatic journey along the same route the day before the outbreak of war in 1939, and then about her difficult but at the same time joyous return to Kraków in 1945, when she climbed onto the roof of the carriage with other youngsters. What did Lili see through her train windows?

Finally I arrive at Victoria Station, crowded as always, filled with the inimitable assembly of London sounds and smells. I take the tube to West Kensington. It's a short ride, I only remove my wide-brimmed Cuban straw hat for a few minutes and then I'm out in the sun again. I cross West Cromwell Road, very busy as always. The air reeks of car fumes. To my nostrils, the smell seems stronger than usual,

*perhaps because of the heat? Or perhaps because I moved
away from London? I walk down North End Road, the
noise of the traffic fading behind my back with every step I
take. At some point grand buildings appear on my left,
opposite a tree which – I can only imagine – must look lush
and beautiful when covered in spring blossom. What a view
from a window to have, in the middle of the city! Before I
turn left, I walk past a corner shop selling the biggest
watermelons I have ever seen. I turn left again and enter a
gated estate furnished with a stunning, manicured garden. I
am early, so I find myself a bench there, in the shade, by the
far wall. I want to sit down and wait. I want to compose
myself. I am nervous, uneasy. I will be talking to a
Holocaust survivor about her war-time experiences, about
her lost childhood.*

*One minute before the arranged time I get up and gather
my things. I leave the garden, and approach the door of an
imposing 1930s building. I press the intercom button and
introduce myself in Polish. A lift takes me upstairs, to level
six. There is a long corridor stretching to the left when I
emerge; it is filled with light. At the end of it a door cracks
open. A petite, grey-haired lady with a smile bigger than life
welcomes me into her home. It is a home filled with things,
with souvenirs, books, records, but more than anything else,
it is filled with pictures and photographs; with memories
from a long and not entirely sorrowful life which began with
a short and very happy childhood, quickly followed by a
tragic, turbulent neither-childhood-nor-adulthood time of
in-between...*

I take a seat in the living room while Lili disappears to

make some tea. It arrives accompanied by a delicious home-made apple pie. I confess, I had more than one slice... I will learn on consecutive visits that the apple pie sometimes takes turns with a cherry pie.

In this beautiful, homely place filled with remnants of such a rich life, with objects that hold, contain, are memories, we talk about Lili's childhood, which – as she says herself – lasted only a few short years and ended just months after her ninth birthday. Specifically, on 31 August 1939, the day before the outbreak of the Second World War.

The Stern family in Planty park in Kraków, 1939

Anna Blasiak: You were born in Lwów [now: Lviv] but you didn't stay there very long. You moved to Kraków pretty quickly...

Lili Pohlmann: I was born in my grandparents' bed. I stayed at my grandparents' for two weeks and then we went back. At that time it wasn't directly to Kraków. We went to Bochnia first. My father was a bank manager and they sent him to Bochnia. We had a rented villa there and, I believe, we spent about a year in Bochnia. Afterwards we moved to Kraków and stayed there until the outbreak of the war. Once a year we travelled to Lwów to visit my grandparents. Ever since then I am a *semper fidelis* to both my beloved cities: Lwów and Kraków.

So your childhood was spent in Kraków plus occasional visits to Lwów?

Yearly visits at Easter time. Every year we went to my grandparents for Passover, my mother and I, and then my little brother too, but not my father. He was working and couldn't go. It was quite an adventure, of course, going by train... I loved it, looked forward to it. All through the year I imagined what it would be like, because it was an adventure for a child. Going by train... And it was a so-called "fast train"! I can't tell you exactly how many hours it took to get from Kraków to Lwów – was it five or six hours? The train didn't stop at all stations, but it certainly stopped at the main ones, and one of them was Przemyśl. Both my mother and my father had family in Przemyśl and they all would come out with food, so that "the poor children wouldn't starve, being on the train for such a long time…"

The family were waiting on the platform, one after another, after another, after another. This person brought this, another brought hard-boiled eggs and hot soup. It was great fun, of course. It was very nice. We would stop in Przemyśl for about half an hour or three quarters of an hour, it was the main stopover. And then we would arrive in Lwów and my grandfather would be waiting for us with a horse and cart. It was wonderful. In my family there were many children about the same age as myself. They were cousins, but once or twice removed, because my mother was the only child. Well, my mother was in fact one of eight – she was the firstborn – but the other seven died within a month of birth, and she was the only one to survive. So the children in Lwów were actually her cousins' children; for me they were cousins once removed.

At first, I was terribly unhappy because whenever I opened my mouth they were laughing their heads off and I didn't understand why. I didn't see anything funny in what I was saying, but they were laughing. And they would say to one another, "Listen to her! What is she saying? How is she talking?" They didn't understand me. I might have said *shoes*, but for them they were not *shoes*, they were *meszty*. The language spoken in Lwów was a dialect, while I spoke pure 'Krakovian Polish'. It was awful at first, but after a few days I got accustomed and even started speaking the way they spoke. That was fine, but by the time I got back to Kraków, I had the same problem the other way round!

We always spent Passover with my grandparents. My grandparents were very religious, in contrast to our home. We were secular, while my grandparents were devout. My grandfather would conduct the Seder, the ceremony of the Passover night. He would be all dressed in white, his hair was white and his beard was white. What he was wearing was a special 'Passover robe'. He would recline on the bed, propped up by pillows, as the Bible says one should do on that special night. The reading of the *Haggadah* went on and on. At some point it was my turn to ask what is known as the 'four questions'. I asked these 'four questions' in Hebrew, which made my grandfather very proud. Then he read to us the story from the *Haggadah*, the story of Passover, of the escape of the Jews from Egypt. It took a long time, half the night, and finally we were allowed to have the first bite of food. Oh, the joy of dipping the hard-boiled egg in salty water!

That happened every year, and every year my grandfather asked me, "What would you like? What kind of present would you like me to get you?" And every year I asked for the same thing, for a watch. Somehow, by the time I came the following year, the old watch was gone and I needed I new one. So the next day he would go out with me to choose a watch and I was very happy to get a new one. I loved my grandparents deeply!

You said that your parents weren't very religious...

We were assimilated. I didn't know very much about Jewish life. I mean, I knew I was Jewish, and I knew my parents wanted to go to Palestine to build the Jewish state, but that was pretty much it. My father was an agnostic, but my mother was traditionally Jewish. Whatever she did in the 'religious' way, she did it out of respect for her parents, so as not to upset them, so as not to offend. That's why every Friday evening she lit the candles and prayed. All was as if she were in her parents' home, all out of respect for them.

And every Friday, a parcel from my grandmother was delivered. It contained a *challah,* some *rogaliki* which she baked herself, all sorts of other niceties. Every single Friday, so that we should have it for Shabbat. My mother, on the other hand, would write a card to her parents, always on Tuesday or Wednesday. She would write it in Yiddish and send it in time, so that they would get it by Friday, before the Shabbat.

So you spoke Polish at home?

Yes, at home and at my grandparents' house too. But I also knew some Hebrew. I was in a Hebrew kindergarten, because both my parents were Zionists and wanted to go to Palestine at some point. However the language spoken at the kindergarten was Polish, though we also learnt some Hebrew. We learnt Hebrew songs and prayers. I said my child's prayer at night before going to bed in Hebrew, but other than that everything was in Polish.

What was the Hebrew kindergarten like?

Wonderful! It was a beautiful, great kindergarten. I think I still recognise where it was when I go to Kraków. I can more or less find it. It was a villa with a beautiful garden. I can't say how many children there were, but I was the youngest. I was always, everywhere the youngest and it was terrible from my point of view. I was very young when I started the kindergarten. I think I was three years of age and the rule was that they accepted children from the age of four. I was always a year behind all the other children. The same thing at school. It made it difficult for me, because I had to pass all sorts of tests to be admitted. But somehow I managed and the kindergarten was great fun, I loved it. Many, many years afterwards, after the war, in Israel, I found the teachers and the owners of my old kindergarten. They survived the war and lived in Israel afterwards. What a happy occasion that was!

Tell me about your friends from the kindergarten and the famous 'dupa' story...

There was a boy in the kindergarten called Gabryś (short for Gabriel). He was amazing, really amazing. I think he must have been five at the time, he was at least two years older than I. He had a group of boys around him, for whom he was the king. He would stand there, his hands in his pockets, looking down at everyone. The management couldn't cope with him, he was quite impossible, God bless him, he was totally out of control! They only kept him because he was the grandson of the Senator and highly respected Chief Rabbi of the Tempel synagogue, the great orator, Doctor Ozjasz Thon. The boy was known as Gabryś Thon, although that wasn't his surname. His surname was Rost.

All boys wanted to be in his group and I wanted to be in it too, but I was just a small fish. I asked him once – I don't know how I plucked up the courage to even ask – and he just looked down at me. He gave me one of his sarcastic looks and I felt like I was nothing, nothing at all. And then one day he said to me, "All right, all right, you may join us, but there is a condition. Go home for lunch. When it's all silent – I imagine you're not allowed to speak at lunch, are you? – you have to say this particular word very loudly." And he named the word, which was *dupa* (It means 'arse'). I told him that I couldn't say it. "As you wish. Fine, but no means no. Goodbye." I was devastated. This was my dream! I wanted to be able to do what the boys were doing. I never wanted to play with dolls, I found it so uninteresting! The boys had their games, they climbed trees. It was great fun. Before I went home, Gabryś also warned me, "You know, if you come back tomorrow and you tell me fibs, I'll know that you're lying, I will know, remember it!"

I went home. I didn't know how to do it, how to say it. While I was having soup, I said it quietly into my soup. My father immediately asked, "Did you say something? What did you just say?" "No, nothing, it was nothing." "Yes, you did say something. What was it you said? What *did* you just say?" Oh my God, it was terrible! So I said, "Well, I had to say it, because Gabryś told me..." "Who is Gabryś? What Gabryś?" he wanted to know. "Gabryś at the kindergarten. You know him, everybody knows Gabryś." "So what did he want you to say?" "I can't repeat it." "You have to. What did he want you to say?" And so, I said it! You can't imagine the commotion at the table, my father to my mother... No, it was my mother who said, "Where are we sending this child?" Nobody referred to me by name, I was 'the child'. "Where are we sending this child? What kind of a kindergarten is it where they use such language? What language is this for a child to use?"

The following morning I came to the kindergarten and Gabryś stood there, as usual, with his hands in his pockets, looking down at me with the quirkiest smile. "So?" he said to me, "You know what? I think you said it!" "Yes, I did. And I said it TWICE!" "Oooh, all right, all right, come, you can join us now."

You impressed him!

I did indeed, but how he impressed me! Oh, he impressed everyone. Now, talking about Gabryś... I have often thought about this boy when I was older, after the war. I was sure he must have survived, he was such a tough cookie. In 1945 a Jewish Committee was created in Kraków, *Komitet Żydowski*[1]. The few of us who survived met there. People were coming back, from camps, from hiding and other places, and their first steps were to the Committee, to look for other survivors. One of the people running the Committee was a female doctor, I forget her first name, but she was 'Doctor Rost'. In 1945 she took down my

---

[1] The Central Committee of Polish Jews, also referred to as the Central Committee of Jews in Poland and abbreviated CKŻP, was a state-sponsored political representation of Jews in Poland at the end of the Second World War. It was established on 12 November 1944 and provided care and assistance to Jews who survived the Holocaust.

testimony, which is published in a book called *The Children Accuse*. I gave the testimony of survival. She was Gabryś's mother... But I had no idea then, no idea. And I kept looking for him under the surname Thon...

I knew more or less what his age would be and I kept asking around, "Have you any idea? Have you ever seen him? Do you know him? Have you heard of a boy called so and so?" Nobody knew anything.

Years later, I used to go to Kraków twice, three times a year with my husband Peter. Whenever we were there, we invariably went to the Jewish cemetery, where I put a symbolic plate for my family members who had perished in the Holocaust, and for my beloved mother, who died years later in London. On one such occasion, instead of leaving the cemetery the usual way, we took a different route. As we were walking along the main thoroughfare there, at the end of it, I noticed from afar a huge black tablet. I said to Peter, "That's very interesting. Let's have a look. What is that?" It wasn't an old tablet, it was something that would have been erected more recently. We came closer and it was a symbolic tablet for the Rabbi Doctor Ozjasz Thon. It said all about his life and at the very bottom this special inscription said, 'And to his beloved grandson Gabriel Józef Rost, born in 1928, who was tortured at Montelupich[2], and perished in a

---

[2] The Montelupich prison (the name is derived from the street where it is located, *ulica Montelupich* or the Montelupi Family Street) is a historic prison in Kraków from the early 20th century, which was used by the Gestapo in the Second World War. It is widely recognised as one of the worst Nazi prisons in the occupied Poland.

death camp in Bełżec[3] in 1942.' Gabryś would have been 13 or 14 years old...

I could not believe my eyes. This boy, so tough, so self-assured... How could he, how could they...? And suddenly it dawned on me that it might have been precisely because he was so tough that he would not have given in, and was tortured like the older ones. He was just two years older than I was. 'Tortured at Montelupich, perished in a death camp in Bełżec in 1942.' I couldn't get these words out of my mind... This was a terrible shock for me and from then on, every time we were in Kraków, we lit a candle for him at the Jewish Cemetery in Miodowa Street.

One day we were going to Kraków, like we used to, and a friend of my mother's and mine got in touch with me, "Lili, I wonder if you could do me a favour? I have a very close friend in Kraków who is not doing very well right now. Would you take some money for her from me?"

I said, "Certainly, of course." I telephoned this lady in Kraków, we met and we spoke. She was a very charming, very nice lady. She said, "When you come again to Kraków, please call me. It would be so nice to see you again." I promised to do that. So next time I was going, I asked my London friend if she wanted me to take something for her friend in Kraków again, and again she gave me some money for her.

---

[3] Bełżec was a Nazi German extermination camp built by the SS for the purpose of implementing the secretive Operation Reinhard, the plan to eradicate Polish Jewry, a key part of the 'Final Solution' which entailed the murder of some six million Jews in the Holocaust. The camp operated from 17 March 1942 to the end of June 1943.

I called the lady up. "Would you like to visit me at home?" she asked.

"Gladly."

We made arrangements, I came. She lived in a very old building, it was a cold, rather neglected, huge apartment. As we were sitting, having tea, I asked, "How are you coping here in this big apartment, all on your own?" She wanted to know if I would like to see the rest of the apartment.

She took me around and eventually we came into a room with a small painting on the wall, a watercolour of a child. "Is that your grandson or a family member?" I asked. And she replied, "Oh, no, it's a terrible story with this one." "What do you mean?" "Well, you wouldn't know these people, you wouldn't know… This boy was the only son of a very close friend of mine, Doctor Rost." "Doctor Rost?" I said. "I knew a Doctor Rost, here, in Kraków." "Well, that was her son, Gabryś." "Gabryś? What Gabryś?" "That was Doctor Rost's son," she replied. And I said, "I knew a Gabryś, Gabryś Thon." "Yes, that's him. He was the grandson of Rabbi Doctor Thon." "So how is it that he is hanging here? Was he a relative?" I would never have known, I would never have recognised him from this watercolour. "Ah, you knew him? How did *you* know Gabryś? He was such a difficult, impossible child!" "Yes, I knew him, we were in the kindergarten together. I knew him, I knew him very well. He was older than I was, I looked up to him. Please tell me how you came by this painting? Were you related?" She said, "No, not at all." I wanted to know more, so she said, "I'll tell you. This picture came from someone who used to look after him. She was his nanny, I think. And, somehow, she got hold of this painting of Gabryś. When she was liquidating her property years after the war, she didn't know what to do with it and, as I was the friend of the family, she asked me if I would like it. I said yes, so she gave me the picture. You see, this lady I got it from was the person to whom Gabryś was handed over by his mother, his parents, to be taken away by her from Kraków, somewhere to the countryside, to be hidden."

Watercolour of Gabryś Rost

He didn't want to go, he was vehemently refusing to leave, but the lady said she would take him and look after him until he could be reunited with his parents. However he was quite impossible. He simply wouldn't go, but eventually they forced him to get on the train with this lady. The control arrived, a conductor walked into the compartment with a Gestapo officer and they wanted to see papers, the usual thing.

"Are there any Jews here?" they asked and everybody said, "No, no Jews here," but Gabryś got up and said, "I am a Jew." They took the boy away, and that was it. That was it. At the age of 14 they were torturing him at Montelupich. What could he have done to be tortured, other than put up a fight, not to give in? So very much Gabryś…

And this is the story of Gabryś, Gabryś Rost.

The lady in Kraków asked me, "Would you like to have the painting? Would you like it? I'll give it to you." "Yes I would love it, but I'm not going to take it off your wall now." I thought if I did it, it would show, the wall would have looked horrible. So I said, "One day… But if you'll allow me, I'll take a photograph of it…" I did, and among my souvenirs, I found that photograph of a watercolour of Gabryś, my childhood hero.

You spent three years in the kindergarten and then you went to school?

It was maybe three, maybe two and a half years… I can't tell exactly. Eventually my father decided that I should go to school. I was six years of age and that was too young at the time. You started school at the age of seven, so everybody was asking, "How do you intend to send her to school at the

age of six? What school will admit her at the age of six?"
And all he said was, "They will. She will get into a school,
and not just any school. I want her in a very special school."
Which wasn't easy. I was too young, I was Jewish and the
school he had in mind was a Catholic school. The name of
the school was St Scholastica School No 1. There were but
a few Jewish girls in the entire school. I had everything
against me. But my father was insistent. He used to say, "A
child who can read, write and count a little, should not be
at home." And he forced it through. I was in front of a
committee and they accepted me.

So when did you learn to read? Did you learn on your own?

My father taught me. We read together, we sang together,
we did many things together with my father. He taught me
proverbs. I learned everything I knew from him...

What was your relationship with your father like?

Fabulous. I was 'daddy's daughter', no doubt about it. We
did absolutely everything together. He took me everywhere.
By the time I was four or so, he would take me with him,
even when he went on a business trip, or for a bank
inspection out of Kraków. I went to Tarnów with him. I was
not at school yet, so I must have been four or five at the time.
He decided to take me with him and I remember these
discussions, my mother saying, "How can you take a child
along? What will you do with her while at work?" And he
just said, "It's not a problem. She has a nanny. She will go

with us and when I'm free, we will be together. I'm taking her with me." He took me everywhere. We danced together, we sang together, we skied together, we swam together, we rode bicycles. Not only did I cycle, I had to do the figure of eight at the age of three or four! He made me do all these things. We went skiing together and, small as I was, I skied between his legs! It was marvellous, it was really marvellous. He was so wonderful. So young, so full of fun. And determined. He wanted me in that particular school and no other would do. And he got me in!

I remember my days at school and what kind of school it was. We had to wear a special type of uniform with white overalls on top of it, and if there was a slightest stain on it, we were punished. We wore slippers with the soles lined with felt, so that we weren't heard and wouldn't scratch the beautiful, shiny parquet floors. That's the sort of school it was.

I remember that there was a priest who came for the girls' religion lessons, and I was then outside the classroom for the duration of the period. We, the Jewish girls, had a Hebrew teacher, or was he even a rabbi? He taught us 'Judaism'. I remember him sitting, eating raisins, and falling asleep. These were the lesson we had. Eating raisins, asking questions, and falling asleep.

We went to some impoverished homes and brought all kinds of things to give to these people. We sang a lot of patriotic songs. It was a very, very patriotic school, and I was proud to be its pupil. When I returned to visit the school after more than half a century, one of the teachers said, "Please, may I take you to the library. It hasn't changed at all since your times." And, true enough, it was just as I remembered it. I realised it as soon as I walked in. Nothing else really changed at school either, except for the great noise of the pupils in the corridors – something that was taboo in my days.

I was always quite good at writing. Since I was very young, teachers praised my writing. No mistakes, grammatical or otherwise. I liked to write and the teacher always had something pleasant to say about my composition. Contrary to mathematics, my writing was always praised by teachers, then and in later years too. Sometimes they would even put my composition on the wall.

Did you have friends at school?

I had one or two friends in my class, but they are no longer alive. Most perished in the Holocaust. One of them was Anita Lampel, with whom I was friendly. I thought she also would have survived, like Gabryś, because she had light blue eyes and she was blonde. So I thought she stood a chance, they both stood a chance to survive. It must be four or five years ago when Peter and I went to Kraków and saw our dear friend, Professor Aleksander Skotnicki, at his workplace in the hospital. He showed us one of the special albums that he had put together and said, "Look at this, this is another person I was looking for." And he showed us a photograph of a lovely, blonde lady. And then he said, "Except that unfortunately she died two months ago, in Canada." Her daughter sent him the photograph. He showed it to me and I exclaimed, "This is Anita Lampel. My

God, she was my friend from school!" I don't know whether there is anybody left still from my school days. Maybe, maybe not. Would anybody even as much as remember me? Why would they, after so many years?

Did you ever experience any antisemitism at school?

I believe I did, yes. I believe that it was an antisemitic incident, though it wasn't called that. Nobody called me anything unpleasant to my face, but this teacher actually hit me. Here's what happened... During the priest's periods at school, I was outside, together with the three other Jewish girls, Anita Lampel, Erna Rainer and Alina Wassermann. I had no idea what went on inside. As far as I was concerned, they were having a religious lesson. What did I know?

On one occasion it so happened that just prior to the main school recess, the teacher gave me a letter in an envelope and told me to go downstairs, to the office, and give it to the headmistress. So I ran downstairs, delivered the letter, and as I was coming back, the bell rang, which meant that everybody had to leave the classrooms. I think we were on the second floor. By the time I got upstairs, they were all outside, on the corridor. The rule was you had to take your breakfast with you and eat it outside the classroom. I went into the classroom to get my breakfast. Not so much for myself, because I never really ate it, but there were two girls from a very poor home who never brought any breakfast from home. Maybe their parents did not even have any to give them? So they were waiting for me to give them my breakfast. I went into the classroom, got my breakfast and gave it to them, all as usual.

The next period was with the priest, so I stayed outside, as always, and after that it was a Polish lesson. As we sat down, the class teacher, called me out. She said, "Stand up." I stood up. "What were you doing in the classroom during the main break?" "I came to fetch my breakfast." "What do you mean, you came to fetch your breakfast? Why didn't you get it before?" "Well, you sent me with the letter. And by the time I got back everybody was outside, so I went in to get my breakfast." She said, "You are lying." "Lying? I'm not lying! I took my breakfast and in fact I gave it to—" "You're lying!" I replied, "I'm not lying!" I had no idea what she wanted of me! She said, "Come out here." I came out. I was standing next to her and she said, "I'm asking you again. What were you doing in this classroom when there was nobody there? What were you doing there?" I said again, "I came to fetch my breakfast." "You're lying. You were reading the sins of...," and she mentioned the name of one girl. When the priest was to come, the girls had to prepare 'to confess' and they kept their 'sins', written on a piece of paper, in their desks. But I had no idea what she was talking about. I didn't know anything about any 'sins', I didn't know what it meant. I had no idea what this was about. I said, "I did not." She became more and more irate, and said, "You took them out from the desk and you read them." I said, "I did not. I just took my breakfast." Then she lost her temper and hit me. I flew straight into a corner. I started bleeding profusely from my nose, my eyes swell. It was terrible, really unbelievable. I had no idea what she wanted from me. How would I know about somebody's sins? What sins? How would I know?

What did your parents do?

When I got home, my mother nearly fainted when she saw me, because my eyes were swollen and the nose was bleeding. I must have looked really bad. My nose got slightly fractured, it is still visible now. My mother was in shock. It was just before lunchtime and my father was about to come home. When he saw me, he thought I had an accident. "What happened? What did you do to yourself?" he asked. I told him and he couldn't believe it. He said, "What? Come here and tell me again. Tell me everything exactly. And tell me the truth. Did you do what the teacher said you had done?" I said, "I don't know what she wanted. I have no idea what it is she wanted of me. She was talking about some sins. I don't know what that is. I came for my 11 o'clock breakfast." "And you are telling me the truth? You *are* telling me the truth?" he asked again. I said, "Of course, I'm telling the truth!" So he said, "Okay, I'll deal with this." And he dealt with it. It went all the way to the higher educational authority, if memory serves me right to Professor Stanisław Skrzeszewski, who, I believe, after the war, became the Education Minister in Poland, but at the time he was the head of the School Inspectorate. And I was again in front of some committee and had to tell the story over and over again, until they believed me. The teacher apologised to me in front of the class...

What was it like with her afterwards?

Very nice. She invariably praised my work. She would sometimes even say, "You see? Lili never makes mistakes." At times she would even show me as an example. That was before September 1939, just before the outbreak of war. I did not go to school afterwards again, because the war broke out.

So who invented this incredible story about you reading the list of somebody's sins?

Well, it was obviously the girl... Why did she do it? No idea. Why would she have done it? She must have hated me because I was Jewish. How would a girl of – what – eight or nine years of age do something like that? To invent such a story? She must have heard something at home, to make her even think that way. I have wondered about it many times. I would have liked to have met her and confronted her. I would have liked to have asked her some questions. Did she remember this event? What made her do what she did? Would she do it again today? But most importantly, what made her do it then? It was preconceived, it was not something spontaneous, she must have thought about it and she must have wanted to find a way to do me some harm.

Isn't it often the case that behind antisemitism you have some absolutely ridiculous stereotype, a made up story?

Absolutely, exactly! How would a child of that age know about antisemitism, if she didn't hear it at home? She must have hated me because she knew I was Jewish. I don't know what makes a child do that to another child? And to make up a story that I went into the classroom to read the list of her sins! It wasn't that anything was lying on top of the desk, no. We had desks which you had to open. These things were inside the desk.

Sometimes I see her surname in Kraków. Maybe it's a relative of hers? Or maybe she is still alive? Would she even remember this episode? Who knows? But to do a thing like this, to invent such a story, and to go to a teacher, to tell her about it before the lesson started? Because the moment the teacher came into the classroom, we just stood up and we sat down, and she called me immediately...

Did you observe any other cases of antisemitism in pre-war Kraków?

Yes, I did, but at the time I didn't know what it meant. *This* is a vivid memory... When Piłsudski[4] died in 1935, we lived at Pijarska Street, which is by the Floriańska Gate in Kraków. Our windows overlooked the walls of the Barbican. When the funeral cortège was passing through the Floriańska Gate we could see it from our windows. And the moment the cortège went by into Floriańska Street and

---

[4] Józef Piłsudski was a Polish statesman who served as the Chief of State (1918–22) and First Marshal of Poland (from 1920). He was considered the *de facto* leader (1926–35) of the Second Polish Republic as the Minister of Military Affairs. After the First World War he held great power in Polish politics and was a distinguished figure on the international scene.

towards Rynek (Old Town Market Square), a policeman on the other side was beating up a bearded man with a truncheon. Beating him up. It was a terrible sight. We were standing by the window and my father was holding me and explaining everything about the cortège and the funeral. And then I saw it. When I saw the incident, they wanted to move me away from the window, so I would not see it. "Why is he beating this man? What has the man done?" And my father couldn't really tell me, so he said, "I don't know, I don't know, maybe he..." But my mother said, "Well, he's Jewish." I couldn't understand, "What do you mean, he's Jewish? Why is he beating him for being Jewish?" My mother realised that she shouldn't have said that. Nobody spoke about it ever again, but this is what happened. I was shocked. I couldn't understand why the policeman was beating a man who was Jewish? That story stayed with me.

When I came to London in 1946 on a communal visa, we were distributed to various families. They had to be kind of guarantors for a child. I was being guaranteed for by a family who lived in Stamford Hill, which is a very Jewish district in London. I knew nothing about that. I was there only for a few days and then I was taken to a boarding school. But I did spent a few days there. On the second or third day, I asked if I could go out and have a look around the area. They agreed. So I went out. It was a main street somewhere in Amhurst Park. On the opposite side I saw a Jewish man dressed in religious attire, something I haven't seen in ages. There was a policeman next to the man. I just stood there, by the entrance door to my hosts' house, and I was waiting for the policeman to start hitting the Jew. He didn't, and I kept waiting and waiting. Nothing happened. Finally the policeman took this elderly Jewish man by his arm, brought him over to the other side of the street, saluted and went off. I couldn't believe what I saw. What was that? Was he a real policeman? Why didn't he beat this man up?

I can see it as if it were today, as if I were standing by the window in Kraków and the policeman was hitting the Jewish man with a truncheon. I couldn't understand that the London policeman doesn't have a truncheon or other weapon. That he is just standing there with his hands at the back and then he takes this elderly man across the street, salutes and goes off. I couldn't believe it was possible. To me, at that time, it was something unheard of – a policeman, to me, was there to beat you up, not to help you.

You described your relationship with your father. What was your relationship like with your mother?

Very good, but different, because my mother was a completely different kind of person. My father was a very sporty, lively man. I am like him, and my little brother was like my mother: fine, noble, elegant, always invariably *comme il faut*. You could have put him in a chair, left, cooked a meal, come back and he would still be there. My mother and my father were opposites.

My mother was a beautiful, elegant and very serious person; my father was handsome and great fun. They were dramatically different from each other – but what a loving couple! My mother would always reprimand me, tell me to behave. Oh, how she suffered my constantly bruised knees, covered with plasters. She was just such a beautiful, noble person. And so was my brother, the replica of my mother, in looks and every respect. I am like my father, in looks and temperament. My mother stayed the same until the end of her days. And there was I, in so many ways her very opposite. She used to ask, "What are you going to do when I'm gone? How will you cope with life without me?" What a wonderful mother she was, what an outstanding person, so clever, so wise. My father too was wise and highly intelligent, but at the same time a fun-loving sportsman, a great dancer. All my mother's girlfriends were in love with my father... Nowadays, when I see Federer play, I am reminded of my father. All my young friends loved him, because he loved doing things with us, and for us, children. He was just great fun, he was fantastic! And so very young! He was only thirty-six years of age when he perished in the Holocaust.

You said your brother Uriel was more like your mother. So would he participate in those activities with your father as well?

No, of course not! He would sit there and read. "What are you doing there?" "I'm reading." "What do you mean, you're reading?" Everybody laughed. "Reading? Right, you are reading, are you? You are five years old and you are reading?! Well, how about you read something to us?" And he did! He taught himself how to read. And not only in Polish, but also in Russian. We never knew how and where he learnt it.

He kept reading all sorts of incredible books. Under the Soviet occupation, we slept in one bed. He always had some amazing books under his pillow, books on biology, mineralogy. Nobody knew where he got them from. He was known as the 'little gentleman', a beautifully mannered boy. People loved him and happily invited him over to their homes. And when he spotted an interesting book, he asked if he could borrow it. People laughed, but agreed. He brought the books home, put them under his pillow and read them at night, a torch under the pillow for light.

And chess? He played chess with grown-ups. They would ask for him. No-one knew where and when he learned to play...

He was always serious. When he was playing outside, every few minutes he would go under the window and call, "Mummy, mummy?" "What is it, Uryś?" "I love you, Mummy." He was a very gentle child. Who knows what he might have become, had he lived? He certainly was a brilliant child.

During the war we all shared a room. When he was getting undressed to go to bed, he folded all his clothes beautifully and in the order of how he would get dressed the following morning. Nobody taught him that, nobody asked him to do that. That's just the way he was.

He was born in 1935, so this was just before the outbreak of war when he was three. There was a big storm over Kraków and he was very frightened. He hid under the table and was really scared, so I held him. When the storm passed, my mother took him and as the sun was coming out, she put him close to the window and said, "You see, Uryś? There's nothing to be frightened of. Sometimes a storm happens. The rain comes down, we need the rain, the trees need it." She explained everything to him. "And sometimes a storm happens." It was difficult to explain it to a three-year-old. "And afterwards the sun comes out, so all is well, nothing to be afraid of." "Where does the storm come from?" he asked. My mother said, "From up there, it comes from heaven." And he says, "Heaven? What is in heaven?" "God is in heaven." "Mummy, have you ever seen God?" he asks. "No, nobody ever sees God. Nobody has ever seen God, but He sees us all. And that is good, because he watches over us." The boy thought about it for a moment, "But, Mummy, if you have never seen God, then how do you know it's a he and not a she?" He was three years old! He was an incredible child, in every respect.

What was Kraków like and what was Lwów like in the 1930s? How do you remember those cities?

I loved both these cities. Lwów – now Lviv – was great fun, because when we were there, we were visiting our grandparents. It was such a lovely city. For me going there was an adventure. It was wonderful, people seemed happy, and full of laughter and music. We had parties, we saw each other after a year's absence. The streets were always full of people. People were singing. It was great fun, the city was very beautiful... It is still beautiful today, though somewhat ravished by war years.

Kraków was my home town and I loved it! I still love it today. My Kraków, my beautiful city... I knew it inside out.

Even as a child I could go out in Kraków on my own and play at Planty[5]. There was music playing in restaurants and in coffee houses. It was wonderful. I loved this music and I wanted to go and dance like other people did. I had a wonderfully happy childhood. What was not to love there, in my beautiful Kraków? What was not to love?

But it took you over fifty years to go back to Kraków...

It took me more than fifty years. I left it in 1946 and I went back in 1998 or 1999. It took me so long for obvious reasons. I had nothing to go for, I had no-one to go to, absolutely no-one, neither in Kraków, nor in what was now Lviv. In 1945, while the war was still raging in Europe, we went back from Lvov to Kraków with my mother. It was terrible for us to be there. We never went anywhere near the houses or the streets where we lived before the war. We lost absolutely everyone. It was just my mother and I, still miraculously alive, so why would I have gone to Poland? To whom? For what?

Eventually I did go, but if it hadn't been for my much loved friend, Rafael Scharf, known as Felek, I might have never gone... He was a *homo cracovians,* a great Krakovian, who spent the war in England, where he was in the army, but loved Kraków until his dying day. A *persona grata* in Kraków, he was very well-known there by all. Everybody

---

[5] Planty is one of the largest city parks in Kraków. It encircles the Old Town where the medieval city walls used to be until the early 19th century.

loved Felek. And he was trying to persuade me to go to Kraków. But my mother would never go, never, so I didn't go for two reasons. What for and to whom? But primarily I couldn't do it to my mother – to go on my own and leave her here? I never did that. I never left my mother on her own. Even though she was much younger then and had many friends here, but no, there was no purpose, no reason for me to go.

So how did he manage to persuade you?

He simply told me me that he himself had been going to Kraków since a few years before and people here held it against him. They said, "Why do you go there? Why? They hate you there. Why do you go?" Nowadays everything is globalised. You don't talk about specific people, you talk about *the* Poles, *the* Germans... "They hate you. Why do you go there?" To which he replied, "Nobody hates me." And then he said, "I'm going because there is a yearly festival of Jewish culture there now[6]." When I heard that, I said, "Jewish culture? In Kraków? What kind of a festival is that? For whom? Where are the Jews?" He started explaining, he told me about the Centre, that there was a Centre for Jewish Culture there now, a truly wonderful centre[7], and "you

---

[6] The Jewish Culture Festival in Kraków is an annual cultural event organised since 1988 in the once Jewish district of Kazimierz in Kraków by the Jewish Culture Festival Society. The main goal of the festival is to educate people about Jewish culture, history and faith, which flourished in Poland before the Holocaust.

[7] The Judaica Foundation was created in 1991, but the idea for the foundation was established already in the 1980s, influenced by the

should see it." Felek was not just anybody, he was a writer, he was a great personality, very well-known and a highly respected person. So I said, "Listen, you tell my mother. I can't go, I can't, because she would never understand why I'm going." And he said, "Fine, I'll tell her." He told my mother about the Festival and the Centre. He said that it would be very interesting for me to see it all. And my mother said, "All right, go with Felek." And that's how it happened!

When I was on the plane with Peter and suddenly saw Kraków underneath, I started crying, and there was no controlling me. I couldn't stop for hours. I cried and cried, and cried. All these years came back!

Some friends were waiting for us at the airport, one of them was this very nice young person from Kraków, who helped caring for my mother, and who always asked me to come to Kraków. I told her that I would come one day, but I never had. So when I was eventually coming, she and her husband couldn't wait to receive us. I was in such tears that I could hardly see who was there. We were staying at the Grand Hotel, but her husband wanted to do something special for us and took us through the street where we used to live, by our house. That was the end, I couldn't control myself, I sobbed and sobbed, it was terrible.

That first trip was like that for a bit. It was incredibly moving, I couldn't believe I was in my beloved Kraków, I

President of the Jewish community of Kraków. Committed to preserving the Jewish heritage in Kraków's old Jewish district of Kazimierz and to opening up a new platform for intercultural dialogue, the Foundation also aims to spur interest among young people in the Jewish culture and history.

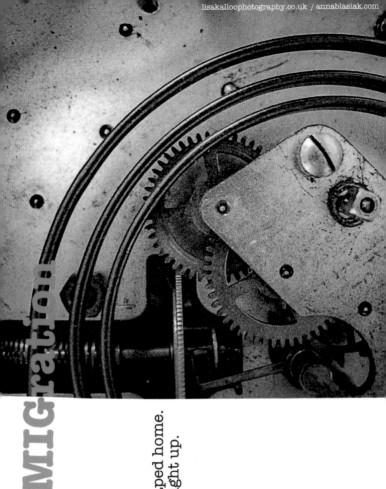

EMIGration

I escaped home.
It caught up.

Emigration
by Anna Blasiak,
translated by Marta Dziurosz

Photograph by Lisa Kalloo

Dear James,

a copy of "Lili" – thank

you for your

help with the

book.

All the best,

Anna

lisakalloophotography.co.uk / annablasiak.com

From the forthcoming book
Café by Wren's St James's Church, *Lunchtime* / *Kawiarnia przy St James's Wrena w porze lunchu* by Anna Blasiak and Lisa Kalloo
(Holland House Books / Stowarzyszenie Żywych Poetów K.I.T. 2020)

LOTTERY FUNDED

Supported using public funding by

**ARTS COUNCIL
ENGLAND**

simply couldn't believe it. I had Kraków in my heart all these years. Kraków lived in me and now I was there again. I simply couldn't fathom it.

You had it under your skin...

Absolutely. When I'm on the phone, I often doodle automatically. And I always end up with the same thing written down. 'Kraków', completely subconsciously. Some people draw something, I invariably put down the word 'Kraków'. Every single time, completely subconsciously....

Lili's primary school, St Scholastica School No 1 in Kraków

Historical Context
1930 - 31 August 1939
Clare Mulley

Lili was born in the vibrant, multicultural city of Lwów in 1930, over a decade after the First World War had restored Poland's independence and her home-town had ceded from Ukraine. After Marshal Piłsuski's death in 1935, the Polish government became increasingly authoritarian, unemployment rose, and the scourge of anti-Semitism intensified across the country. In Germany, the Nazi Party had already seized power, enshrining their anti-Semitic policies into law. Within a few years, the Third Reich had annexed Austria and the Czech Sudetenland.

As borders began to close in 1938, Britain offered sanctuary to 10,000 unaccompanied Jewish children mainly from Germany, Austria, Czechoslovakia and Poland: a significant but small fraction of those under threat.

Poland had treaties with both the Soviet Union and Nazi Germany, but was unaware that under the Molotov-Ribbentrop Pact, Stalin and Hitler had agreed secret plans for the partition and occupation of Polish territory.

CHAPTER TWO
WAR. LWÓW-LVOV-LEMBERG. GHETTO
31 August 1939 – 18 November 1942

Anna Blasiak: I am fifteen, I live in Poland. It's 1989, the year of the Big Change in my part of the world. I am too young to vote, but I can sense the political fervour which is simmering around us. The air smells of it, it smells of change. But... Change from what to what? The new, glimmering on the horizon, is only marginally more interesting than the old, older still, not just my times, but times long before me. Because what was *before?*

At school I learn a bit about the history of Poland, about – as we are told over and over again – its rich and diverse history. About settlements of Muslims (Polish Tatars who came to these lands in the fourteenth century), about Eastern Orthodox Christians, about Lutherans and Calvinists as well as other Protestant groups, like members of the Unity of Brethren, fleeing their homeland and settling in Poland in the sixteenth century. And, first and foremost, about the Jews.

I am told stories about them arriving in what was to become Poland as early as in the tenth century, then again in the following centuries, when they were fleeing persecution in other parts of Europe (in Germany in the fourteenth century, in Hungary in the fourteenth-to-sixteenth and then the seventeenth-to-eighteenth centuries, in France in the fourteenth century, in Austria, Spain and Portugal in the fifteenth century). I am taught about the fourteenth century Polish king Casimir the Great who welcomed the Jews with open arms and created a safe haven for them in the Polish lands. I am told about how tolerant and accommodating Poles were, welcoming the newcomers, their elder brothers in faith. I learn about the peaceful coexistence, about Poland as Paradisus Iudaeorum, *as the Jewish historian Samuel Adalberg called it. I am also told that this synchrony of Poles and Jews goes on up until the Second World War. Not a word is mentioned about the sixteenth century ban on new Jewish settlements or buying properties in prominent locations, nothing about religious conflicts starting in the second half of the seventeenth century, nothing about the nineteenth and twentieth centuries pogroms, which continued even after the Second World War. According to my teachers, Jews lived in Poland in absolute peace, respected and appreciated by fellow Poles until the Holocaust came and the Nazis wiped them off the face of the earth. The end. No Jew survived in Poland.*

That's *what I'm taught at school.*[8]

This is not something that families talk about either. I can't quite understand why. Why is it a hush-hush subject? I try asking my grandparents about the pre-war Poland and about Jews whom they must have known. They must have met them in the streets of their towns and villages, they must have shopped in Jewish-run shops, had shoes fixed or

---

[8] Since then the national curriculum has changed and more is taught about different attitudes of Poles towards Jews.

clothing made by Jewish cobblers and tailors, drank at Jewish-run inns, been treated by Jewish doctors. My father's family comes from a village near Mogilno in central Poland. The first Jews settled there at the end of the eighteenth century. The synagogue in Mogilno was built in 1902. My grandmother was born in 1914, just a few years later. Many local Jews left there after the First World War, but whoever remained, was murdered in 1939 by the Nazis. My grandmother was 25 at the time...

My mother's family also comes from central Poland, from a village near the town of Ślesin (or – what is probably a clearer geographical reference for most Polish people – near the village of Licheń, with its famous miraculous icon of Virgin Mary and gargantuan basilica built recently in her name). By the time I start asking questions about Jews, my mother's father is already dead. And my grandmother doesn't want to talk about it. At some point I find my way into the attic in her house where I discover a collection of books in German. All I am told is that, yes, a German family lived there at some point and then they had to go away. I later find out that at the end of the nineteenth century a quarter of the population of the nearest town, Ślesin, was Jewish. That there was even a Yiddish-language theatre there. Most of Ślesin Jews perished in the Holocaust, but two families escaped in the 1930s and ended up in Argentina.

Why do my grandparents on both sides refuse to talk about it? Why do they dismiss me and silence my questions? Why this reserve and total denial? All they say is in line with what I hear at school – that Jews lived here, yes, and now they are gone. End of story. Nothing to talk about. And yet occasionally I hear some derogatory word, something that only at some point I realise is in fact antisemitic. I don't understand... Where does that come from? What do they mean and why do they say those things? Who are they talking about?

1989 is also the year when I finish primary and start secondary school. I am now considered mature enough to be allowed to travel on my own. Well, a little bit. And so I do. Every year for my winter holidays I go to Kraków. It's a long journey from Słupsk on the Baltic Sea coast, where I live. It takes twelve hours on the train, often with no seat, just standing or sitting down on the floor in the corridor, or by the loo. The trains are so overcrowded that sometimes to get in, you need to climb through the window, followed or preceded by your luggage. In my case it is a huge navy-blue rucksack with an aluminium frame. But all that hassle is worth it.

I spend days wandering around the city of Kraków. It's grey, not only with this standard, Polish People's Republic's greyness, but also with a different shade imposed by winter. The city is half-deserted, it's drab. Yet it is beautiful. I can see the beauty even though everything is crumbling, falling apart.

I can't even remember how I ended up in Kazimierz for the first time. It is an old Jewish quarter of Kraków, once a separate city, established by King Casimir the Great in the fourteenth century and named after him. According to the legend, the root of King Casimir's benevolence towards the Jews was the soft spot he had for his Jewish lover Esterka. In the early 1990s Kazimierz is even more drab and grey than the rest of Kraków. I go from synagogue to synagogue. Closed, boarded up. I visit the Jewish cemetery, abandoned and disintegrating. I walk the streets, push gates which sometimes give in and allow me to peek into enclosed yards. Everything is filled with the silent scream of absence.

Several years later I am a student of art history in Warsaw and, together with a friend, I travel around south-eastern Poland. In my friend's little car – I think it was a Cinquecento – we get to some pretty remote places, small towns and villages. The usual scenario goes like this:

There is a large building somewhere quite centrally located, completely abandoned, doors boarded up, windows broken. Often the building is on a plot of land that is fenced off and overgrown with greenery. Around the perimeter of the fence life goes on, but inside only pigeons and probably rats persist. Local people never venture there. They treat this blot on the map of their town or village as if it simply weren't there. When asked, they go quiet. They don't want to talk about this building. They know nothing. They don't want to know. And the building? It's of course a synagogue, a remaining physical proof of rich Jewish life that once thrived in these parts. Possibly one of the last pieces of evidence still there...

A large synagogue is a bit harder to ignore than tombstones from Jewish cemeteries placed face down and used to pave the roads. Or broken into smaller pieces and used for foundations of new buildings. Or turned into whetstones. But memory is not just in people, it hides in things too. Disappearing things take the memory with them...

Other buildings, homes, apartments, shops, as well as

land and smaller pieces of property, were simply (and quickly) taken over by the Polish neighbours. And now nobody talks about it, about those houses with holes where mezuzas used to be fixed to doorframes, about those buildings, those roads. About the synagogues sometimes turned into shops or sports, or cultural centres, about the overgrown cemeteries where cows or goats graze. It's a rare thing to find a plaque informing about the Jewish history of a particular building or place, like in Sierpc, where the building of a funeral parlour was a Jewish butcher's before the war. Everybody looks away. Is it shame? Shame for something the people did or didn't do? There are stories of Polish people who did help the Jews during the war and later kept very quiet about it, afraid of their neighbours... Or was it shame because of what/who they were/are?

*Polish troops marching to the Western Front
to meet German invaders*

*

Anna Blasiak: On 31 August 1939 your father put your mother, you and your brother on a train going to Lwów. That was the beginning of the war for you, wasn't it?

Lili Pohlmann: That was the beginning of the end of my childhood, the end of my happy childhood. 31 August 1939.

It was just you, your mother and your brother, but not your father. Was it because of work that he didn't come along?

Even then nobody anticipated that the war was so close. We knew it was coming. Everybody knew that. The war, the war, the war... People were escaping, going east. But that it was going to happen on that same night? Nobody anticipated that.

My father put us on the train. My mother had just her handbag, that was all. I don't think she even took any food with her. There was no way of getting anything with us onto the train. The train was so full that to get onto it was a miracle. My father had to put my little brother through the window. People were hanging outside, on top of the train...

We were as we stood. My father said through the open window, "Don't worry, I'll take care of everything, I'll pack and send things via a transport agency to Lwów and I'll see you in two days' time." But when he got home, there were call-up papers waiting for him, even though he was category C, which was a low category. He was category C, because he had a problem with his knee since he was a young man. We had no idea he got called-up, because there was no communication any more.

*Why do you think he decided to put you on the train on 31
August?*

I don't know why, I don't know. He was planning to send
us off to Lwów anyway. The war was in the air, it was any
minute, any moment, but nobody expected it immediately,
there and then, this minute, that day. He did say, "I'll see
you in two days' time." But of course he didn't and we had
no idea what happened to him. The war started on 1
September 1939. The Germans bombed Lwów[9] very early in
the morning, around five or six o'clock. Everything
happened so quickly. He was called up to the army and
fought around Kielce, I believe, until the army was
disbanded and there were just a few of them left from his
whole regiment or division. And he made his way on foot to
the city which by then was called Lvov, but that took a long,
long time.

By the time he got there, Poland was divided between
Germany and Soviet Russia, the Soviet Army had taken over
Lwów, and so we were under the first Soviet occupation. He
walked over 300 kilometres almost barefoot. When he
arrived, he looked... Well, we didn't recognise him, we
didn't know this man with a beard, disheveled, barefoot,
who was standing at the door. And we had no idea what

---

[9] The city was called Lwów when it was part of Poland, before the
war. Under the Soviet occupation the name changed to Lvov. Then
it was Lemberg under the German occupation (like previously,
when it was the capital of the Habsburg Kingdom of Galicia and
Lodomeria at the end of eighteenth and in the nineteenth century).
It then turned back into Lvov under the second Soviet occupation
and is now known as Lviv.

happened to him. We didn't know that he was at the front. "I'll see you in two days' time…" and then silence.

What was the journey itself like? How did you experience it as a child? How much were you aware of, actually?

I was aware, because everyone around talked about nothing but war. But what did I know about the war? That there was going to be a war, war, war, war. That's all I knew. We were on holidays then, near Bielsko-Biała, in Podlesie, and my father cut it shorter because of the imminent war. So we came back to Kraków about ten days before we were supposed to. That was my awareness of what was going on. I knew it wasn't going to be fun. People were talking about it, they were coming, and they were sitting and planning. You know, people plan and then… Suddenly the men were taken to the army. Many went eastwards, like we, whether to Lwów or not, but eastwards, away, as far as possible, to Ciechocinek, towards Romania. People were escaping. It was havoc. I felt things were not good, but that was all. I don't know whether I felt fear. I don't think so, but I certainly was aware that this was it, that we might have to escape, and maybe we would come back, or maybe we wouldn't. And then my father and my mother decided that we were going to Lwów. Her parents lived in Lwów and that was more than many people had. Many had nobody there, they were just going eastwards, hoping for the best. We had somewhere to go, we had somebody to go to. In hindsight, I see it was an enormous advantage. So my parents decided that my father was going to send us off first and he was going to sort out some things, prepare and send whatever was necessary to us to Lwów, but that never came, everything stayed behind. That was it. I never saw my home town, my house, my home again… Until almost 60 years later.

The journey was of course much, much longer than in normal circumstances, because the train stopped in every small town and village, to take on more and more people. We went to Lwów every single year for Passover on a fast train, so I knew that the first stop, I believe, was Przemyśl and then I'm not even sure if it stopped anywhere else between Przemyśl and Lwów. It was one or two stops, and that was it.

This time the train stopped frequently, at every little village, and took more and more people in. They were hanging outside, attached to one another, not even to the train. The squeeze in the compartment where we were was unbelievable! I can't even imagine how my mother managed to get a seat. By the time we reached Przemyśl, it was like before – the family were there on the platform, to feed us. Only this time we really had absolutely nothing to eat, this time it was no fun, it was havoc, absolute havoc. People were getting out of the train, into the train. The noise, the shouting, the screaming! It was pandemonium. By the time we reached Lwów, it was about ten o'clock in the evening, which would have been about ten or eleven hours spent travelling, not at all like before. But as it was still summer, it wasn't dark. It wasn't exactly sunny but it wasn't a night just yet. It was sort of semi-dark. And there were soldiers lying on the platform, sleeping. It was something I had never seen before. They were lying there, one next to another, sleeping. It was very difficult to get out of the train because there was nowhere to put your foot down between them on the platform. You had to step almost on the soldiers. I remember it so vividly. It was a very sad sight.

The Germans bombed us that same night, they bombed St Elizabeth's church. And the station. I think, the station was the first to be bombed. These poor soldiers... So many of them perished only a few hours after I saw them there, lying, sleeping... This sight stayed with me for life.

So were they actually Polish soldiers who were called up, like your father?

Yes, of course. They were probably going to be sent off to the front the following morning.

Is that how it was explained to you then?

No, nothing was explained to me. I can't remember anybody explaining anything to me. Who would have the time to even talk about it to a child? This is just what stayed in my memory. It was terrible, because so many of those soldiers perished.

Opposite my grandparents' apartment, there was the main gas station providing gas for the whole city. And apparently, as we learned many, many years later, a bomb fell there too, but did not explode! It was found there many years later, when they were doing some work. An unexploded bomb opposite the house of my grandparents. Now, imagine if that bomb had exploded! The whole city would have been gassed. That's just another little, or in fact not such a little miracle. There are many, all inexplicable, you cannot logically explain them...

Meant to be?

You can call it that, you can call it fate, you can call it coincidence, you can call it whatever you like, you can also call it a 'miracle'. People call it all sorts of things, but it certainly was not something that a writer would have come up with easily. It's inexplicable...

So you, your mother and your brother made it to Lwów just before the war broke out. The war started and you were staying with your grandparents, and then a good few weeks later your father finally joined you.

As I said before, the Russians were already there, in what was then Lvov. It must have been toward the end of September. My father arrived in a terrible state. Up until then he was the young man, very good-looking man, full of life and vigour, a sportsman. And now we had before us a man who was broken, completely broken. He had nightmares, he was talking and shouting in his sleep. It was horrendous. His looked changed, he had this wild look about him now, it wasn't the same person. It really was heartbreaking to see, for me, for my mother, for all of us, for my grandparents too. To make things worse, he had fought before in the Polish-Bolshevik war in 1918-1920, and since then he had an absolute abhorrence for Bolshevism and

Bolsheviks. He didn't trust them. And here we were, occupied by them. So it was a tragedy for him.

His nervous system gave way. He developed very acute pains, which, as the doctors assessed, were all interconnected. The sciatic pain made him almost an invalid. My father – an invalid? It was terrible! He was hospitalised and was being treated with bags of hot sand! It was wartime, there was no adequate medication. While hospitalised, that was the treatment he was receiving. His nervous system, his spirit, they were broken, he was not the father I knew. And on top of it he was under the occupation by the system he abhorred and distrusted, and had to work for them... So, psychologically and mentally, he was at a point of breaking. It was too sad for words to see him that way... I didn't ask any questions though. I knew what happened. He was on the front and saw terrible things. It affected him in extreme. His nervous system gave in.

But everybody had to work, and so did he. Of course not in his profession, because that was 'too bourgeois'. He had to invent a new profession for himself. He decided he was going to be a carpenter. He could always make things with his hands, he was very, very talented in many aspects. He could build a house with his hands. Whatever he did was perfection. Both the Russians and, afterwards, the Germans, admired his carpentry and cabinet making, and they both said the same things to him, "You're not a carpenter." "What do you mean, I'm not a carpenter? Of course I'm a carpenter! It is my profession, that's what I do." "No, no, no, no. You're not *just* a carpenter. Maybe you're a cabinet maker." "Well, yes, I can make things which are perhaps a little nicer, but we don't need such things nowadays, so I'm doing what I'm asked to do. If you want me to do something a little better, I'll do it." "Yes, but you are *not* a carpenter." They respected him wherever he worked, because of his work, because it was just so good.

How about your mother? Did she work?

No, she didn't have to work, men had to work. She was at home and she was doing little jobs here and there, whatever anybody needed, whenever people wanted her to help or sew something.

My parents found a small apartment for us in the centre of town. It was almost palatial: we had two rooms and a kitchen. Of course, no such luxury as water or a toilet. For that you had to go outside. But we were together.

What about you and your brother? Did you go to school?

I did. I loved the school. It was a very good school, the pre-war Maria Konopnicka School, a well-known, very good school. Our lessons were in Polish, with Russian language additionally. They also thought I had some talent for music. You know, in Russia, when they recognise talent, they give you the opportunity to progress. So I was sent to the Music Conservatoire in Lvov and – as I was learning to play the piano before the war – they gave me piano lessons. I was also in a choir and after a while I became a soloist in the choir. They were going to send that choir to perform in Kiev during the holiday time of 1941, but the German-Soviet war[10] pre-empted that and we didn't go. It was a question of a few days. Had it broken out a little later, we would have been in Kiev, I would not have seen my family again…

Wouldn't your family have gone with you?

No, only I. Of course they asked whether my parents would allow me to go. I was very happy that they agreed. While I was at school in Lvov, we were singing, dancing, going to the theatre. It was fine. They brought the Bolshoi[11] to Lvov, I remember. I think it was still 1939 or very early 1940. They came to the Lvov Opera House, which, by the way, on the outside is the replica of the Vienna Opera House. They brought a revolving stage, a novelty in Lvov. The whole town was talking about, "Oh my God, a revolving stage!" And my mother took me to see two ballets. I remember it like today, I can see it in front of my eyes! We were amazed with the revolving stage. So there were some nice moments, but otherwise it was a different story…

---

[10] The German-Soviet War was a conflict between the European Axis powers against the Soviet Union, Poland and other Allies, which lasted from 22 June 1941 to 9 May 1945. It was the largest military confrontation in history, characterised by unprecedented ferocity, destruction, mass deportations, and immense loss of life. As the site of nearly all extermination camps, death marches, ghettos, and the majority of pogroms, it was central to the Holocaust.

[11] The Bolshoi Theatre is a historic theatre in Moscow, which holds ballet and opera performances. The Bolshoi Ballet and Bolshoi Opera are amongst the oldest and most renowned ballet and opera companies in the world.

For children it was fun but for the grown-ups it was a completely different matter. The elites and intelligentsia, not only Jewish, but Polish as well, were hounded – there were round-ups and shootings. Professors, doctors, writers and officers were taken away and killed.

It was also very hard for the evacuees or the people who – like my father – fought in the war. Some of them were on their own, mostly men whose families stayed in the West, on the German side[12]. A lot of them were our friends from Kraków. They knew that we were in Lvov and were coming to us, because we were a family unit, which was a rarity. There were long discussions about what to do, whether to go back or not. In those days people were writing letters from the German-occupied side, saying that it was not too bad, "We're working, we still stay in our apartments." Life went on, things were more or less normal. That was 1939, 1940, 1941. So, with letters like that coming from the other side, people who found themselves without their families, wanted to go back home. They thought the situation was better there than in Lvov with the Russians, the Soviets.

On one particular day three men came to visit, old Krakovians, friends of ours. They came to discuss the situation. There were notices all over the city informing about an agreement with the Germans: anyone who came over from the German-occupied Poland and now wished to go back to their families, should register and they would be allowed to go back. These men came full of joy, "Isn't it

---

[12] The territory of Poland at the time was divided into two zones, one under the Soviet occupation and another under the German occupation.

fantastic? We will be able to go back!" But my father said – and that I remember very vividly – "This is a trap. Don't register, don't do that! It's a trap." "What are you talking about? There are notices all over town!" And he said again, "Don't register. This is not going to happen. I know the Russians. It's not going to happen." They all registered and that same night were taken away and sent to Russia...

My father did not register and we stayed behind. Today I can tell you, oh, how I wish he had registered! I wish they had taken us away. We might have survived, he might have survived, my little brother might have survived! People *did* survive. Yes, many perished, but many survived, too. They were not being killed or murdered, they were there to work, work hard, with very little to eat, in atrocious conditions. In Siberia. And yet, strange, like somehow people didn't require doctors anymore in Siberia? Those who were ill before the war, suddenly were not ill anymore. We were getting letters from those who were taken away, "Please, send us this or that." So my parents were sending parcels to their friends in the depth of Siberia. I remember my mother saying, "How is it that he can eat that now? He was so ill before the war. He had such stomach problems." I remember very vividly this man who would always say, "I don't know if I can eat this, my stomach..." And now he was not ill anymore.

It was a question of survival. You either survived or you didn't, but nobody murdered you, nobody killed, there were no selections in Siberia. In temperatures -40 or -50 degrees you had to work hard, you had practically nothing to eat. We all knew how terrible it was, but there was a chance of survival. And many did survive. As an example, look how many survived and joined the General Anders' Army[13]. People survived, whereas we had no chance. The Germans were very, very shrewd. There were hardly any selections at first. In 1939, 1940, 1941, people were writing letters saying they were not doing badly, so people wanted to go back. however, from the moment the war broke out between Russia and Germany, that's when everything changed. The Ribbentrop-Molotov Pact was broken on 22 June 1941, at the end of June the German Army entered Lvov...

Right before the Soviets retreated from Lvov, your father was offered a chance to escape to Russia with the retreating Soviet forces. With your whole family. He refused. Was that again because he thought it would be better under the Germans?

It was not so much that he believed it was going to be better under the Germans, but because of the distrust and hatred he had for the Bolsheviks. That was the main reason. Despite the fact that he was very well treated at work. He was always respected and greatly admired for his work. His Soviet boss would always stand there and say "Tsk, tsk, tsk. It's absolutely beautiful. How did you do it?" And he would add, "You can't be just a carpenter, you *can't* be a carpenter." Sometimes he

---

[13] The Anders' Army or the Polish Armed Forces in the East was the army created in the Soviet Union, which, in March 1942, based on an understanding between the British, Polish, and Soviet sides, was evacuated from the Soviet Union and made its way through Iran to Palestine. There it passed under the British command and provided the bulk of the units and troops of the Polish II Corps (member of the Polish Armed Forces in the West), which fought in the Italian Campaign.

would bring chocolates and put them in my father's pockets. "For the children," he would say. The Russians love children. There was something very human about the head of the establishment employing my father, there was nothing to dislike about that man. He was the one who said to my father, "I'm going to give you a lorry. Take your family, take whatever you need, whatever you want to take. You have space. Take and go." And my father said no, thank you. The man sent the lorry to our house and said, "Please think again. I'm giving you a chance to get away. You should take it, you will regret it if you don't. You will be very sorry." And my father said, "Thank you, that's very kind of you, but no."

Governor Hans Frank entering Lemberg, August 1941

As soon as the German occupation began, the situation started deteriorating rapidly. Already in July 1941 all the Jews were ordered to start wearing the Star of David...

Pogroms and the infamous Petliura Days[14] followed immediately. Apart from the German occupiers, against the Jews stood the special militia and guards, consisting of Ukrainians, Latvians, Lithuanians, Estonians. There were agonising scenes taking place in the streets, persecutions and beating up of Jews.

In August 1942, as part of the Great Action, fifty thousand Jews were sent from Lemberg to the death camp in Bełżec—

That's when my little brother Uriel and my father perished. On 15 August 1942. There were rumours beforehand about a very specific selection aimed at women and children. Nobody wanted to believe they would take women and children. "Who wants children? What do they want children for?" No-one believed it possible.

Well, your father did believe in the end.

I don't know whether he actually believed it or not, but he thought there might be something to it. By then we already

---

[14] A pogrom of Jews in Lemberg which took place in the last days of July 1941, named after the assassinated Ukrainian leader Simon Petliura. The killings were organised with German encouragement, while Ukrainian militants from outside the city joined the fray with farm tools.

were in several *Aktions*, we were all taken away in several selections. This time my father said, "Right, women and children, they are talking about women and children. In this case, you," he said to my mother, "you and the children have to go into hiding. You can't be at home. I have papers, because I'm working. They won't touch me." My mother said to that, "What? No, no, no. We won't leave you alone. No!" There were quite a few discussions about that, quite heated ones. And then they decided what to do. There was a place next door, it was a shop belonging to two Jewish sisters, who my mother knew. It was a millinery shop. She asked them whether they would take her, me and the boy. "No," was the answer. "Because he's too small, he may cry." My father said, "In this case you will go with Lili, and I will stay and have little Uryś with me. He'll stay with me. I have very good papers, as I'm working." And he wasn't working just anywhere, at the time he was working as slave-labourer for *Sonderdienst*[15], so he had very good working documents.

In the end, it was decided that my mother and I should go, and they would stay. And that's how it was. Unfortunately, our Ukrainian house caretaker brought the Gestapo over, they tore up my father's papers – that's what we understood from the neighbours who saw it happening – and took them away. We were told that they took them to the courtyard outside. My little brother was very fair, blonde, with green eyes, there was nothing Jewish about his looks. Apparently this German

---

[15] *Sonderdienst* (German: *Special Services*) were the Nazi German paramilitary formations created in the General Government during the occupation of Poland in the Second World War.

guardsman wanted to let the child go free, but Uryś didn't want to let go of his father's hand. So they took him away with my father and that is the last thing we know...

While we were in hiding, my mother and I had an arrangement with my father that every day after work, at six o'clock, he would walk past the shop with my brother, on the opposite side of the street. They would just walk slowly, so that my mother could see them through a keyhole, and make sure they were all right. This was the arrangement between my father and my mother. But on that infamous day, on 15 August 1942, they did not walk past. She stood there waiting and waiting. Nothing happened. The shop was closed, of course, the shutters were down. As if this made it a good hiding place! It was absolute nonsense when you think of it today.

Suddenly two women stopped by the shop, leaning against the shop shutters, and started to talk. They were two caretakers' wives, one from the house where we lived, at number four, and the other one from number six, where the shop was. And the one from number four said to the other woman, "You know, the Gestapo came to our house and they took..." And then she mentioned the names... "You know this lovely little boy? Remember this little boy?" And she described my little brother so vividly. And we heard it all. Then the other woman said, "What? You mean so and so?" So she repeated it again, "Yes, you know this little boy and his father. They came and took them away."

At that moment one of the sisters screamed and nearly fainted. My mother and I were like pillars of salt, not a tear, nothing. Shock! We couldn't talk, we couldn't believe what we were hearing. After a while, my mother said, "I'm going to look for them. How could they have taken him away? He had such good papers! How is that possible? I need to go." The sisters didn't want to let her out. It was too dangerous for her to come out of the shop. She had to wait. In the evening she said again, "I am going." She went to my father's work place, to see his boss, the *Sonderdienst* officer, and she told him what happened. He was furious, "What do you mean? How did they dare to tear up my papers? My papers? They had no right to touch him! Come, we are going in a car and we're going to look for them." The *Sonderdienst* officer took my mother and they went from place to place to look for my father and brother. They were nowhere to be found.

What happened, I don't know for sure. Whether they were sent to Bełżec, because, apparently, everyone from that particular August selection was sent to Bełżec. Cattle trains were waiting. Or perhaps something terrible happened to them while still in town, we don't know.

The following day my mother – how naive can one be, and how brave?! – she went back next door to the house we used to live in. She went to see the caretaker, to ask him what happened. As she entered, she saw a man standing with his back to the door. She thought it was my father, because he was the same height, had dark hair, like my father, and was dressed top to bottom in my father's clothes. On his wrist was my father's watch and it was our radio playing... She was in shock. I don't know how she dared to go in and how he didn't do anything to her? He, too, must have been in shock, seeing her...

What did he say?

He said that he didn't know anything. I don't know whether she even told me exactly. She only said that he was standing there, with his back to her, wearing my father's beautiful blue silk shirt I remember so well, and his grey flannel trousers. The caretaker was standing there, with his back to her, so at first she thought that was my father. And then he turned around—

Did she confront him about the clothes and the watch, and the radio?

I don't know, I don't know whether she confronted him about anything, but she must have been in a kind of shock. I don't even know how she got back safe to where we were.

So that summer was like a sped-up growing up for you...

Growing up? I was quite grown up already by then. My childhood ended on 31 August 1939, at the age of nine. We were not children anymore. It was no place and no time to be a child. When I think about it, I can't understand how my mother left the caretaker's home, how the caretaker didn't stop her? All he wanted was my father's watch and the radio. Beforehand, he would come occasionally, knock on the door in a very friendly manner, have a pleasant chat, and then he would say "Oh, Mr. Stern, I like your watch." But if I were to tell you that I like your watch, you wouldn't take it off and give it to me, would you? No, you would say, "Thank you."

That's what you would do. So my father said, "Thank you very much. It is a birthday present from my wife." And then the man would come again and say the same thing. "I like your watch." Eventually my mother said, "Give him the watch." "Why should I give him the watch? Why should I give it to him? Why do you say that?" my father would reply. He couldn't understand that this was what the man wanted. The caretaker would also say, "You know, your radio is marvellous. I love your radio. It's wonderful, it has a green eye. I like this radio of yours. It plays nicely, very nicely."

My father always worked on it, improving things. "How do you do this? How do you do that?" The man was very interested in everything, very keen. And that was that. My father said, "Well, you're welcome to come and listen to it." And my mother said, "Give him the watch and the radio." "Why?" My father could not understand that he should give his radio or his watch away, and so in the end the caretaker brought the Gestapo and got the things he wanted. Simple as that. Who knows what might have happened had my father given him the watch? Who knows?

After your father and your brother were gone, did you go back to your apartment?

It was sealed, they sealed it immediately. We had to join my grandparents, who, by that time, were in the ghetto. At that time the ghetto was not yet completely closed. It was, what they called, 'an open ghetto,' which meant people could go out to work, because there was no work in the ghetto.

What was life like there?

There was no life there. It was horrendous. Three families in one room. I don't know how we ever managed, but we did. We were sleeping one next to another, as I said, three families in one room. My grandparents, my mother and I – that was our family. And then there were two other families. It was terrible. There was no food, typhoid and all sorts of illnesses were rampant, and, of course, selections non-stop. When I say selections, I mean people taken away in transports and constant killings inside the ghetto. Working people were going out of the ghetto in groups, to work outside, and coming back in groups. At some point later my grandfather was taken out of his group and shot on the spot. There were people lying on the pavement, dead. It was horrendous, horrendous. And there was a camp in Lemberg, a concentration camp[16]. The commanders of the camp were the worst of the worst, the cruelest of cruel; that's who they sent to us. They already went through Lublin[17] and through Kraków, and then they came to us. Some had Polish names, like Grzymek and Rokita. These were the heads of the camp. The cruelty of those men and the guards was indescribable. What these men were capable of doing to people in that camp is beyond words. Practically no-one survived that camp...

---

[16] Janowska concentration camp was a Nazi German labour, transit and extermination camp established in September 1941 on the outskirts of Lemberg.
[17] KL Lublin, or Majdanek, was a Second World War German concentration and extermination camp located on the outskirts of Lublin. It had seven gas chambers and was one of the largest Nazi-run concentration camps.

When the ghetto was still open, my mother worked outside, for a civilian German institution. She was assigned a job in a German housing office. It wasn't that she had a choice though. People had to work wherever there was demand. They were 'slave labourers'.

My mother left the ghetto every morning to go to work with her group and came back the same way in the evening. Anybody who dared to stay behind outside of the ghetto and was caught, was finished. Death punishment. My mother was a very talented fashion designer. Now she was a dressmaker. With her exquisite taste, she was always in demand to 'create' and sew. There were three sisters, Polish ladies, who knew my mother from before. They begged her to stay for one evening or overnight, once or twice, to do some sewing for them. They wanted only her. She said, "You know what that means? That means death punishment not only for me, but for you three as well. Why do you insist on having me? You can have anyone else." "Ah, nothing will happen. Please, please, stay for one night…"

They were semi-aristocratic ladies, so their apartment, as you would expect, was accordingly very beautiful and large. Three Italian officers had two rooms allocated in the ladies' apartment. There were some Italian soldiers in town at the time and these officers were occupying rooms in Polish homes. My mother said, "Listen, you've got the officers staying in your place. How do you expect me to come? It's not on." And one of the ladies said, "Oh, is it the Italians you're worried about? The Italian officers? They sing and drink wine all the time, and they really don't care!" But my mother kept putting it off and putting it off. She didn't want to do it, but they kept insisting and so one evening she came back and said to my grandmother, "Look, tomorrow I will not come back." My grandmother knew about these Polish sisters. "They were so adamant that I should stay one night, so, in the end, I gave in. I promised them I would come. They asked me to stay the night tomorrow, so don't worry about me. It'll be fine, I'll be there for one night only and I will see you the following day." To which my grandmother said, "Oh, God, I'm so sorry, because I have managed to get hold of...," whatever it was, I don't know, but it was something to eat. "I know how much you like it, so I got it and I can only cook it tomorrow, otherwise it will go off. I won't be able to prepare it for you the following day, because it'll just go off." Was it some potatoes? It was probably nothing much to talk about, but she managed to get 'something' that my mother liked. My mother, who would never upset her parents in the slightest, minutest thing, felt so sad about it, that she told my grandmother, "Look, in this case I'll tell them that I will come the following night. I won't do it tomorrow, but the day after." And that was that.

On the night she stayed away, a rumour spread within the ghetto that they were closing up all the entrances to the ghetto, and anybody coming from outside from work who did not have the right badge proving that they worked for the military or heavy war industry, would be stopped at the gate and sent directly to Bełżec. My mother, of course, didn't have the right badge, because she worked for a *civilian* German institution. When I heard that, I immediately decided that I must find a way to prevent her from coming back to the ghetto. It was the night of 18 November 1942, the night I escaped from the ghetto in order to prevent my mother from coming back.

First I just waited. Everybody was hiding, because the Gestapo were coming into the ghetto, doing a selection. Where do you hide? Where can you hide? Under the floorboards, in cellars. Where else could you hide in the ghetto? In this particular house we were staying in, everybody also hid in the cellar. But you didn't just go down into the cellar the normal way. Part of the cellar was prepared beforehand. Some of the floorboards could be lifted and you had to go down through this opening. There was a carpet on top of the floorboards. You went down on a ladder and that was the 'hiding place'. My grandparents and I also went down; we were going to spend the night there.

I was in my pyjamas. It was November and it was very, very cold. I had a little jumper on top of my pyjamas and on my feet, a pair of slippers, that was all. My grandmother brought something to cover me with, so that I could sleep. I decided that I should wait until everybody was fast asleep and then try to let myself out. Which was easier said than done, because, beside my grandparents and me, there were many people there from the whole house. So I waited, I pretended that I was asleep and waited, and waited, and waited until everyone was asleep. What time it was, I don't know exactly, but it could easily have been about one or two o'clock. We went down about nine or ten in the evening. I finally heard that my grandparents were asleep. Some of the others were deep in sleep too, snoring. I decided to try get myself up the ladder. I prayed that nothing would squeak, that there was nobody there who was not asleep. It wasn't going to be easy. Still, I got up that ladder and had to lift the floorboards without making a noise. I don't know how I did it, but I did. Nobody saw me, obviously nobody heard me and even if they did, they did nothing about it. I went through the floorboards and put the carpet back down. It was eerie, absolutely eerie.

The silence... The house was empty. It was snowing, it must have snowed just beforehand, because the snow was fresh. Beautiful, white, virgin snow. The moon was shining. Everything was white. It was kitsch. If you saw it in a painting, you'd think – kitsch. I went out and when I started walking, it felt like the whole town could hear me, because the snow was squeaking under my feet. And I was cold, so very cold. I was in pyjamas and slippers... Opposite the house was a railway embankment. I had to get up the embankment to get to the other side, which I did, but the moment I was on the top, dogs started barking from the other side, and there were shots all around me. I fell down and lay facedown in the snow, on the rail tracks. I lay there motionless and waited.

After a while, the dogs stopped barking and there were no shots anymore. I lay in the snow, face down, just like I fell. I didn't move. I don't know how long I lay there, but eventually I decided I would have to risk it. Either I hurled myself down back where I came from or to the other side. I could hardly get myself off, I was getting stuck to the ice, my face, my whole body. It was all quiet, no more shots, no more dogs. So, without getting up, I decided to crawl to the other side and went down like a snowball. And there I was,

I managed, I don't know how. Despite guardsmen and dogs. I was out of the ghetto. I started walking. I *had to* get to my mother and stop her from making her way back to the ghetto.

Were there any people in the street?

No, there was curfew. Nobody, only eerie silence... Not a sound. I could only hear myself shuffling through the snow. And it was white – the snow was white, the moon was white, and I was like a blot on the landscape. I was dark and I was moving. I walked along the longest street in Lwów, by now Lemberg. It's famous for it, it's kilometres long. Kleparowska Street, that's what it was called before the war. What it is called now I don't know. I walked and walked, and walked, and then this thought occurred to me... What am I doing? Suddenly it dawned on me that further up, on both sides of the street, there were German military barracks. And always, day and night, there were soldiers standing guard outside. *Wehrmacht*, regular soldiers. On both sides of the street, one opposite the other. When I realised that, I wasn't sure what to do. That street had no side streets whatsoever, nothing. Once you were on it, you were either going up that way or you were going back, but you couldn't get into any side street, because there weren't any. So what was I going to do? Obviously I would get caught. I was thinking and walking, thinking and walking, and walking and thinking. "What to do? Should I go back now? I'll be caught by the embankment, no doubt. But I've got to stop my mother, I have to get to her to stop her." That was the one thought in my head, I had to get there no matter what. I kept walking and then I saw the two guardsmen. I was very close. I was convinced that either of them, this one or that one, would stop me or shoot me or take me, but I continued walking... Only I didn't get stopped. I walked right past them and... nothing happened, neither soldier stopped me. Then I was sure that I was going to be shot in the back as I went past them. But they didn't. They let me live!

They chose to ignore you? Another miracle—

It was! How else would you call this? I was a child. A child was walking down a deserted street in the middle of the night, so obviously from the ghetto, because there was nowhere else. It was two or three, or four o'clock in the morning, curfew. A child in pyjamas and slippers, in freezing cold, in deep snow... Who was I? It was crystal clear. And they let me go... I walked past them and kept walking and walking on this never-ending street. At the end of it, there was a tram depot. Trams started and finished there. I wanted to take a tram to get as close as possible to where my mother was, to avoid walking in curfew through town. I got inside a tram, which I knew was going to that area where my mother was, and I put myself down in the corner. It was terribly cold.

Shortly afterwards, young men started coming in, workmen, the first workmen going to work. So it must have been five or six in the morning. They started coming, one after another, and then more, and then more, and then more.

Eventually the tram was filled with people. Each one looked at me when getting on the tram, and looked away. As if they didn't see me, as if nobody *saw* me. They looked at me and turned away. The tram was full, a conductor came. "Tickets? Tickets?" He looked at me and turned his head away. Nobody said a word to me and nobody gave me away. They are my unsung heroes, these kind, good, decent people. Nobody did a thing. They all looked away. It really was unbelievable! In those days, if one was not denounced, it was a wonder. We were being denounced left, right and centre. "He's a Jew, she's Jewish." That was enough, that was quite enough. They said, "A Jew!" And somebody took you and shot you. Just like that. And here were all these people, the tram full of workmen, ordinary people, and they never saw me. Just like these two German soldiers standing guard in Kleparowska Street, my other two 'unsung heroes'. They all let me live.

As a Jew living in Lemberg at that time you couldn't know how anybody, any person you met in the street, was going to behave. They could become your instant enemy or your instant hero.

You never knew. We had so many against us in Lemberg, so many who were brought there purposely, to be guardsmen, to be this, to be in the SS. Horrible people, all henchmen. That's why what happened to me is beyond comprehension. How? Divine intervention? Was I meant to survive? But then why I, why not my little brother? Why did he have to die like that? Who decided I was to survive? Who? What? Fate, miracle, coincidence? What was it? You can ask many questions, but there is no answer. The only thing I can say is, 'Here, but for the grace of God...' But if that is so, then, why was God graceful to *me*, but not to... Why would I be the one to live and not somebody else? It's a trauma, a trauma carried by many all life long. One lives a so-called 'normal life', with all that 'normal life' gives and offers you. One has to, one must, otherwise one would go berserk. You try, you live, you do, you see, you sing, you work, you meet people, but, deep inside, you carry with you this perpetual guilt and trauma, the life sentence for having survived.

Lili's brother Uriel in Lemberg, July 1942

Historical Context
31 August 1939 – 18 November 1942
Clare Mulley

The Wehrmacht invaded Poland from the west on 1 September 1939, marking the start of the Second World War. Seventeen days later, the Red Army arrived from the east. When Poland fell, both forces launched pre-emptive strikes against resistance to their occupation, by arresting, deporting and executing many thousands of Polish officers and members of the intelligentsia. The following spring, as the Soviets murdered 22,000 men at sites such as Katyń, the Nazis invaded France and the Low Countries.

Deferring his plans for the invasion of Britain after failing to take control of British airspace, Hitler looked east. On 21 June 1941, he ordered the invasion of Germany's former ally, the Soviet Union. The dynamics of the war now changed dramatically, with Stalin joining the Allies and 'pardoning' surviving Polish POWs and deportees who formed a new Polish Army in the East.

Six months later, while Britain was enduring the Blitz, the Japanese bombing of Pearl Harbour brought America into the war. Despite facing the combined strength of these newly Allied forces, just weeks later, at the start of 1942, senior Nazi officials prioritised meeting to agree what they called the 'Final Solution' regarding Europe's Jewish communities. Polish Jews had already been confined to ghettos. In May 1942 alone, 300,000 were transported to Auschwitz. Many more were sent to other Nazi German extermination camps in occupied Poland, such as Bełżec and Treblinka.

CHAPTER THREE
FRAU WIETH
19 November 1942 – November 1943

*

Anna Blasiak: We make decisions every second of every minute of our lives; some are big, of great consequence, and some so small and insignificant we don't even register them. But what does it take to make a momentous decision to help another human being who is in danger? To do something that might save their life, especially when that decision means putting your own life in jeopardy?[18] I want to believe that I would do the right thing, that I would be the 'good person', but how can I know, really?

Irmgard Wieth helped Lili Stern and her mother by hiding them in her apartment for over a year during the German occupation of Lemberg. She was German and worked for a German civilian organisation. She didn't really know much about the fate of the Jews. Or rather, she knew the bare bones but not the details. She was one of those who accepted that the Jewish people were there to serve the Germans. She didn't question anything that was going on around her: Jewish workers coming from the ghetto every morning and going back for the night, being worked like slaves, some of them suddenly disappearing... Well, she didn't question anything for a while, up until the time when

---

[18] Poland was the only German-occupied territory where a person helping Jews was punished by death, along with his/her family.

she met Lili and her mother and got to know them better...

In Poland the antisemitism was widespread too, in part instilled by the Catholic Church, which put centuries of hard work into building this division, feeding and fuelling it. Fortunately history also knows cases when representatives of the Church did the right thing and helped the Jews. But during the war some Polish people, just like a lot of others, happily looked the other way when something was happening to the Jews, those – as they were repeatedly told by their priests – 'killers of Jesus Christ and of small children for blood for matzo bread.' And even if they didn't act against them, they were quick to take over their property as soon as the Jewish owners were out of the picture. There are stories about Polish families unexplainably gaining houses or land, about expensive pieces of furniture mysteriously finding their way into peasants' homes. About unanswered questions about their origins. These objects, things left behind and taken over not only contain history, they are its witnesses.

Frau Wieth was brought up in an antisemitic home back in Germany and, even at the time when Lili and her mother were staying with her, she still repeated some antisemitic statements she had learnt from her father. However she was able to transcend the antisemitism drilled into her. She quickly started seeing fellow human beings in the Jews she was helping and decided to cast her father's teachings aside.

Despite her indeed heroic actions, Frau Wieth never considered herself a hero. Quite the opposite, in fact, she thought she was a coward. She wasn't seeking recognition or awards. She was very reluctant to talk about what had happened during the war. When – on Lili's and her mother's initiative – she was being awarded the title of the Righteous Among the Nations in 1967, she had to be tricked to even come to the Israeli Consulate in New York. It was as if she wanted to forget the whole thing had ever happened. Perhaps that was the way of dealing with her initial antisemitism that she was brought up in, but also with doubt and fear for own life (she planned to jump out of the balcony should the Gestapo arrive to arrest her)? Perhaps it was easier to deal with all those emotions by forgetting. As if one ever could...

Polish writer Zofia Nałkowska famously said that 'People prepared this fate for people'. As in, 'bad people' did it to 'good people'. The question is though, is anybody ever entirely 'bad' or entirely 'good'? Nobody is just one thing...

Frau Wieth, as Lili always calls her, arrived at her transcending decisions slowly, through ritual like repetitions. Three times she was asked by Lili's mother to help them before she finally said yes. Three times she visited the Lemberg pharmacy to ask about a companion for Lili when the girl threatened to run away back to the ghetto. This process of arriving at a decision, of switching from one position to its opposite – because nobody is just one thing – this ritual that it sometimes entails, makes me think of fairy tales, of sending protagonists on three dangerous missions with three tasks to fulfil before they get their reward...

I consider all this looking at the world as it is now, during 'the war' on coronavirus in early 2020, when we are all in a crisis situation and in self-isolation, as Lili was for most of the time she spent at Frau Wieth's apartment, sometimes even locked-in to prevent her escape. And like Lili, whose survival strategy at some point was to pretend to be a German girl when out in the streets of Lemberg, I too feel like a chameleon, with my identity shifting from moment to moment, and not just between two languages, two homes, because I may be British, but my Polish accent betrays me the moment I open my mouth. And now, in the coronavirus times, new lines of ebbing and flowing emerge. Stuck at home, the 'outside facing' side of things goes into longer and longer suppression and hibernation periods, while the 'inward looking' self takes over more and more. Lili's chameleon game took place in the chameleon city. The pre-war Polish city of Lwów became Lvov under the first Soviet occupation, them Lemberg under the German occupation, then Lvov again, and finally Lviv, as it is known in Ukrainian now. However Lili pretty much always remained 'Lili' (with a small exception, when she was in the Greek Catholic orphanage and was known as 'Lidka'). But, after all, nobody is just one thing.

Passport photo of Irmgard Wieth

*

Lili Pohlmann: I found my mother in the Polish ladies' apartment and told her that it was impossible to go back to the ghetto. What to do then? First of all she said, "We have to go now, I have to go to work." She took me with her to work. Well, when I say she took me with her... To say it is one thing, and to do it was quite another thing. To go with me through town looking the way I did... To say it was a little awkward is to say nothing. And she had to be without an armband, as Jews were not allowed to walk around the city on their own. The difficulties were excruciating, but we got there somehow. The others, the whole group of workers from the ghetto arrived, unaware that on their way back they would be taken, because they did not have either the required 'W' or the 'R' badge. Just that small patch of fabric was then a lifesaver...

They arrived and were all busy working, while I put myself in some small corner of the room. Suddenly a German woman walked in, very tall, very lovely-looking, a beautiful woman. She approached my mother and discussed what my mother was sewing for her. They talked, and then suddenly she noticed me. She pointed her finger at me and said, "*What is it that?*" Not 'who'. I was a 'what'. "*What is that?*" she repeated. To which my mother replied, "This is my daughter." "Oh," the woman said rather matter-of-factly. "What do you mean, this is your daughter? I thought your son was dead." Just like that! "I thought you said that he was dead." Very calmly my mother said, "Yes, you're right. I had a younger son, and he is indeed not here anymore, but this is my daughter." "Oh," she looked at me again, turned around and walked away.

Anna Blasiak: How much did you understand from this exchange? At that point you didn't speak German?

No, I didn't. I only saw and I understood some of it. I did understand some German, I just didn't speak it. I had no opportunity to talk German to anyone. When she said, "What is that?", I knew. And, of course, I looked like a 'what'. I mean, I must have looked quite a sight. When you imagine that I was covered with snow before, and with ice, and I was in my pyjamas. What did I look like? The 'What is that?' was not really that surprising...

After a while the German lady, who was called Frau Irmgard Wieth, came back, and again said to my mother, "When are we going to have a fitting?" My mother replied, "We are going to have a fitting in a few minutes. And I would like to ask you to take me to a different room for the fitting." The lady kept looking at me, but didn't say anything else. She didn't make any remark about me this time, nothing, just kept looking. My mother followed her to a different room, and while they were having this fitting, my mother said to her – just imagine the courage she needed to say what she did! – she said to the German lady, "As you saw, I have my daughter here with me. She escaped from the ghetto. You know that I have already lost one child and I absolutely must spare this one. Would you help us? Would you take us in for a few days only, just for the duration of this particular selection?" A Jewish woman saying this to a German, who had just come up with the 'What is that?'... Frau Wieth said, "Do you know what you are asking of me? How dare you say anything like that to me?! To suggest such a thing! *Do you know* what you're saying?" "Yes, I do know. I know, but what am I to do? We have nowhere to go and I want to spare this child." The German woman didn't say anything in response. They finished the fitting, my mother came out and then Frau Wieth came out. Nothing happened.

After a while she came back again to the room where everybody was working. My mother worked among other people. The German woman came and said, "You mentioned that we need another fitting. Do we indeed need another fitting?" My mother confirmed, "Yes, we will have another fitting." "I'll be ready in about 15 minutes or so." And so it was, she came back and again they went together to another room. Frau Wieth didn't say a word. She was just being fitted. My mother did what was necessary, and then turned to her again, "I'm asking you again. Would you *please* help us? Would you take us in just for a few days? I promise that the moment this selection is over, we'll go back to the ghetto, it's just for now."

Three times this happened. The German woman didn't say anything. Again she came and looked at me. She just looked at me and looked at me, and went out. And then, during the third fitting, she said, "Right, I'm leaving here at five o'clock. I shall be walking with so and so," and she said with whom. "With him and his secretary. The three of us will walk together, then we'll part our ways at a certain spot. I'll go my way and they'll go their way. You will be walking a considerable distance behind me with your daughter. Quite a distance behind me. And that's it. Five o'clock." *And that was it*! We had to hide from everybody, so that they wouldn't see that we were not going back to the ghetto. It was terrible! What could we do? We followed the woman.

It was November, it was freezing cold and snowing. At five o'clock it was dark, night-time already. We did exactly as she said. The three of them walked together and then they parted their ways. We followed her and arrived at the house where she lived. She told us the number of her apartment, the floor and everything – where, how and so on. She was on the third floor. We had to be careful so that nobody would see us. We walked up the stairs. We didn't want to risk taking the lift. Nobody saw us. We were lucky, we were simply very lucky. She opened the door and we went in. There we were! Entering that apartment was like getting into paradise! As I said, it was November and November can be very, very cold in Poland. And suddenly we walked into this warmth! The flat was centrally heated. It was a brand new apartment building, built just before the war, very modern, light, bright and centrally heated. So we walked into this warm, beautiful, clean, wonderful apartment. Coming from the ghetto, from such terrible squalor, we were... in paradise. We could not believe that this was happening to us! And yet...

My mother said to the German lady, "I promise you that the moment this selection finishes, we'll go back, we will not impose upon you, not for another minute, but for the time being, please will you try and listen out to what's happening around?" Frau Wieth had no idea about what was going on in town. All those civilian Germans lived in a bubble of their own. And Frau Wieth not only lived in the 'German' district of Lemberg, but in the 'SS and Police' district, and the house she was in, was requisitioned for high SS and *Schutzpolizei* officers and their families. She lived there, because at some point in the past she had had a boyfriend who was a high ranking SS officer. It was in fact his apartment. When he was about to be sent away from Lemberg to Holland to run a Jewish concentration camp, he told her to stay in the apartment. And she stayed. "You have to listen and watch," my mother stressed. "When you find out that the selection is over, that everything is quiet again, we'll leave."

Frau Wieth went to work each morning and while she was not in, we were not allowed to move *at all*. There was a parquet floor in the flat, no carpets, just a beautiful parquet floor. And immediately below us, lived the Head of the Ukrainian Police with his family! He was the only non-German in the building. So we were not supposed to move, otherwise we might be heard, and we knew what that meant... Sitting in one place, we couldn't even go to the toilet. How did we do it? How did we manage? Not to move until she got home from work. Then, once she was back, we were allowed to move a little bit, but slowly, one at a time, *never* together.

This went on for a few days, and then one day Frau Wieth came home and said, "I think it's over. It seems the selection is over." My mother said, "Well, in this case we'll go back. If you are one hundred per cent sure... But what I will require is an 'R' or a 'W' badge in order for me to be able to get back into the ghetto. Where do I get it? How? Didn't you mention that you still have a Jewish doctor?" my mother asked. (The woman believed in Jewish doctors and Jewish pharmacists. This particular doctor was still

95

practising at the time and she remained his patient.) My mother continued, "If you could ask Doctor Schwieger to get you an 'R' or a 'W', I will pay for it whatever it costs and then we can go back to the ghetto." "How am I supposed to do that?" "When you go to see him, just ask him. What can we do? We have no other way. There is no other way."

So Frau Wieth went, and indeed she asked him. The man, of course, was stunned. He thought it was some kind of a trick. "What do you mean? Why would *you* need a thing like that?" She was a very naive person, very naive and very straightforward, upright, honest. What she thought was on her tongue. She didn't know how to lie. So when the doctor asked, she told him, "Well, it's because I have a Jewish lady and her young daughter with me, and they want to go back to the ghetto." She told him the whole thing! The man stood there and couldn't believe what he was hearing. He said, "All right, I'll try to get it for you." And he did! He got my mother an 'R' badge, 'R' for the heavy war industry. 'W' stood for *Wehrmacht* and 'R' for *Rohstofferfassung*. When he was giving it to Frau Wieth, he said, "You know, we don't have children, my wife and I, but I have a niece. She's 18 years old. Would you take my niece and hide her also? For which I will pay you," and he named a large sum of money, in dollars. "I will provide food and pay you." Frau Wieth refused, "No, I'm sorry, I can't do that. They are going back to the ghetto. I can't continue with it." She came home terribly upset, in a real state. My mother was concerned, "Why are you so upset? Has something happened? What is it?" Frau Wieth had great respect for my mother. My mother spoke fluent German and they communicated intelligently. Frau Wieth was a highly intelligent woman. So she told my mother what took place at the doctor's. "But why are you so upset?" my mother asked. "What do you mean, why? How did he dare to *offer me money*? If the Gestapo were to come... Well, my conscience is clear – I wanted to help. But to do a thing like this *for money*?? To die at the hands of the Gestapo *for money*? How did he *dare* to suggest this to me? I don't do that sort of thing for money!"

She was terribly irate and greatly upset about the whole incident. "If I have you and Lili here, and they get me – well, I tried to help and got caught. But *to die for money*? Never!" My mother comforted her, and said, "Please, calm down, I understand." And added, "I have the badge now, so we shall leave tomorrow. When you come home from work tomorrow, when it's dark, we'll go." To which Frau Wieth replied, "You know, Frau Stern, you don't have to leave. You can stay. I'll have you here with Lili. You don't need to leave." "That's impossible," my mother said. "First of all, I promised you that we would go. And secondly, I have my parents – I hope I still have them – in the ghetto and I need to go and look after them. I can't just not go back, we have to go. You are too kind, too wonderful, but we'll go. And thank you, thank you very, very much."

Frau Wieth said then, "You know, Frau Stern, you are a grown-up person. You can do as you like. I can't stop you. If you don't want to stay, you can go. But Lili, *I will not give you Lili.*" To which my mother said, "What do you mean, 'you will not give me Lili'? What do you want to do with her?" "No, I will not give you Lili, she will stay here with me." "That's not possible! How can you do that?" And Frau Wieth said, "I will not give you Lili because..." You see, her words are difficult to translate into English, maybe even impossible to translate, to convey the special meaning. She said in German, "*Für Gestapo ist mir Lili viel zu schade*," which, roughly translated, meant, 'It would be too much of a pity to let Lili get into the hands of the Gestapo.' "But I want you to know that if they catch you, you don't need to worry about Lili. I will adopt her..." And that was that.

How old was Frau Wieth then?

She was two years younger than my mother and my mother was born in 1906, so Frau Wieth would have been 34. She was young, beautiful, very special. You can see it even in her passport photograph, the one I had enlarged. That's the only thing I had of hers. I still have it. This is what she looked like, the passport photograph was taken, I think, in 1941. She resembled the actress Katharine Hepburn. When she lived in America after the war, in New York, people were stopping her in the street. She looked so much like the actress. Ever since we knew her, she even wore her hair in the same fashion.

Do you think she was maternal towards you?

I really don't know, but she did love me. She never was the one to embrace or kiss me, no, no, no, but she was very fond of me and somehow she admired me. She admired the fact that I learned German so quickly and so well, that I could write well. She always used to say, "Nobody in the whole world is like Lili." And she would start a long list of adjectives. When my daughter Karen was born, Frau Wieth would later be saying the same about her. Only Lili and Karen... She thought highly of me, but I don't remember her ever embracing or kissing me. Not even in later years. It just wasn't her thing. But, in her own way, she loved both of us, all her life long. I might have been the nearest thing she had to a child... And she was always full of admiration for me, which made me feel very embarrassed, particularly when she sang my praises in front of others.

In those days I didn't realise what an extraordinarily fine person she was. But if she hadn't been, would she have kept me? Endangered her own life? It was all so amazing. I didn't even speak any German at first, I could not communicate with her. It was my mother who did, not I. I just sat there and when she said something to me, I would only say, "*Ja*," just in case, and not too often either.

So in the space of a few days in her eyes you went from 'What is that?' to 'Für Gestapo ist mir Lili viel zu schade'?

Yes, and to 'but Lili I will not give you'. It was quite extraordinary! She didn't know what an average Jewish person went through, she only saw the slave labourers. They were there to do things for the Germans. And that was normal for her, I think. We never discussed that. And the civil servants, ones like her, did not mistreat these people. They were working for them and that was it. All these Germans knew was that the Jews came, worked and went back to the ghetto. But they were in fact *slave* labourers, they were slaves.

To Frau Wieth it was normal, she didn't question it. And then suddenly she realised that Jewish people – like my mother and myself – were also human beings. She realised that we were no different to anybody else. Not once or twice did she say to my mother, "You know, Frau Stern, you are not Jewish, you can't be Jewish." My mother was fair, had green eyes, had no mannerisms that were obviously 'Jewish'. She was a very calm person, she never panicked, always very logical and practical. Whenever anything was happening, she would say, "Please, I need a little bit of calm around me. I need to think." And Frau Wieth admired that greatly, she admired my mother, she had great respect for her. Not that she showed it in any specific way. She liked to talk to my mother and she repeatedly said, "You're not Jewish." Which made my mother laugh, "What do you mean, I'm not Jewish?" "Well, you can't possibly be Jewish!" "Why can't I be Jewish? Why? Have you ever seen a Jewish person in your life?" "No," Frau Wieth said. "So how do you know I'm not Jewish?" "Oh, you can't be, you don't look like a Jew, you just can't be Jewish." "But think for a moment, just think. Why would I be here? Why would you be hiding me from the Gestapo if I were not Jewish?" "Ah. Well..."

Frau Wieth was a very decent, but equally naive person. What was on her mind, was on her tongue. Her traits of character, her principles were very firm, honest, upright, trusting. At the same time, she was an eccentric... 'Eccentricity' could have been her middle name.

But also, she was not necessarily very empathetic —

For us she had a lot of empathy, but heaven help if somebody said something to her, which she didn't think was correct or honest! But if you were honest and decent, she respected you. She was also a very shy person. That shyness stemmed from the fact that she was very tall and striking-looking. When she was walking, she walked with a straight back, her head up, which made her seem even taller. Because she was striking, people were looking at her and she didn't like that. It made her feel uncomfortable. In those days you didn't see women of such height. And in her high officers' boots, she looked taller still. And she had that 'sporty' look about he, and that's why she loved what my mother created for her: no frills, simple, elegant, the way she liked it, the way she was.

Did she ever talk to you about her family?

I knew about her mother and father, about two aunts, that's all. Later, I found out that she had some other relatives, I think a nephew. She also had a brother, who died. I'm not sure whether he died during the war or after the war. And that was it, nothing else. I do believe that she might have had a child once, because there was a birth certificate of a child at home, a birth certificate of a little boy. He would have been approximately my age. I believe he died in infancy. I can't remember the name. My mother and I never asked her questions. After the war there were even more reasons not to ask. I didn't want to refer to those days not to make her feel embarrassed about anything that might have occurred during the war, so I never asked. And she never volunteered anything, except about her mother and her two aunts. I knew about her mother, because I was writing letters to her mother. Frau Wieth would lie on the couch and I would be on the floor next to her, and she would dictate her letters to me. I would write for her, to her mother, to her aunts... In Gothic script, because this was what I learned from the books in Frau Wieth's library. When I was on my own, books were the only thing to occupy my mind with, and that was how I learned to read, write and to speak German. She was very happy, she didn't have to do anything. She was always tired after work, because she hated her job. She was not an 'office person', she disliked it. But I didn't know it then. I just knew she would come home and say, "Oh, I'm so happy to be home. And I'm so tired." I would run a bath for her and then she would lie down. "Oh, how wonderful!" And she would listen to the radio.

Do you remember where in Germany her parents lived, which part of Germany?

I knew where her mother was. Her father wasn't alive anymore. He had been a university professor, I believe, and a great antisemite. That was what she said. During their discussions, my mother would ask her, "Have you ever seen a Jew? How do you know what a Jew looks like?" "No, I haven't," Frau Wieth would reply. "But my father told me those things." It was her father who taught her hatred for the Jews.

So what happened after Frau Wieth's doctor got your mother an 'R' badge?

My mother went back to the ghetto and I stayed. My poor mother went back late on the Sunday night, it must have been before ten o'clock in the evening. Curfew... She needed to get herself into the ghetto. For me it was horrendous, because I never knew whether I would see my mother again. She left wearing old peasant clothes and a thick peasant shawl, so huge she was completely wrapped in it. You could hardly see her face. That's how she walked through the entire city, from one end to the other, in curfew. The ghetto was on one side and we were in the German section of the town, which was a new district on the opposite side of Lemberg. First she had to get to the place where there was a Jewish group coming back from work, try to join this group and put the armband on. I never knew whether she was alive or not. For the whole week I had no idea. She would come back on Saturday evenings, stay one night and one day with me, and go back on Sunday night. That's how it was until the ghetto burned down and she escaped, from November 1942 to the end of May or beginning of June 1943. It was indescribably difficult for me, to endanger my mother this way, and I didn't want to stay without her. I felt tremendous guilt that I was in such comfortable conditions, while people in the ghetto were dying in the streets. I did not want to be at Frau Wieth's. I wanted to be in the ghetto, with all the others.

When your mother came to see you every weekend, did she tell you what was going on in the ghetto?

Of course! I wanted to know about my grandparents, about everything. And I really wanted to go back with her. Or escape from Frau Wieth's and get into the ghetto on my own. I told Frau Wieth how I felt and, as a result, she started locking me up. When leaving the apartment, she would lock the door from the outside. There was a balcony in the apartment. I would lie down flat on it and see groups of Jews going to and from work down below, passing by. I decided I was going to write a note and try to get it down to them, hoping that somebody might pick it up. I wrote, 'Would you please see if such-and-such a person is alive. When you come back just nod. If you nod, I'll know it's a yes.' It was very risky. On two occasions people managed to find my mother and the following day I saw a nod from one person in the group. I don't know who it was. So I had some information, but I still wanted to go back to the ghetto. Frau Wieth knew that and was very upset about it. She didn't know what to do.

One day she came home and said, "Don't worry, you'll have company." "I'm not worried. What company?" I had a shock. I asked, "What have you done? What do you mean by 'company'?" There was a well-known pharmacy in Lemberg and at that time it was still managed by the same Jewish man, Mr Podoszyn, who had managed it before the war. "I went to the *Apotheke*," she told me in all her naïveté, "and I asked the Jewish manager if he knew anybody who I could take in, so that you would have company." Can you believe that? His reply was, "No, I don't know anybody." Times were hard, everybody was scared. And here comes this German woman... The man didn't think she was crazy, but he thought it was some kind of a trick. So she went there again. It was like with my mother...

She went to the pharmacy again and again, and she said, "Listen, I'm still looking for somebody. I need somebody because I have a Jewish girl staying with me and I need some company for this girl." That's what she kept telling him and he would reply, "No, I don't know anybody. I'm sorry." But when she came for the third time, he said, "Okay, I have my wife and she's here, in the cellar. Would you like to take her?" And Frau Wieth said, "Yes, I'll take her right away." He brought his wife out and Frau Wieth brought her home. She was a very lovely lady, and Frau Wieth was satisfied that I would not run away now, because I had company. Within one week the pharmacist himself – the lady's husband – decided to join us too, without even asking! He just came one day. And then there were *three of us*. Frau Wieth was now hiding three Jews! Some Ukrainian was bringing food for the pharmacist and his wife once a week. Frau Wieth was not aware of this. She never wondered where they got food from. If she knew, she would have thrown them out. She would have seen it as something done behind her back, she would have perceived it as dishonest towards her, something she would not tolerate.

She shared her rationed food with me. She even wrote to her aunts in Germany, who ran a confectionary shop, to send her lemons, sugar cubes and chocolate. They didn't know it was for me, but they did send such parcels. Small parcels would arrive and they were for me. I would squeeze lemon juice over sugar cubes, and so, I was never hungry. But she also shared her food with me.

When I was with Frau Wieth still on my own, at some point food was practically non-existent, so whatever rations she had, the two of us shared them. Once she brought some potatoes home and I thought, "Okay, what should I make with the potatoes? How about potato pancakes?" So I made potato pancakes. I prepared them before Frau Wieth came home from work, so that she could have them for a 'surprise dinner'. I fried the potato pancakes directly on the stovetop, because we had no oil or frying pan. She loved them! They were very nice, nice and crispy. And what did she do afterwards? She went to work the following day and, I imagine, had a chat with her co-workers. "What did you do last night?" somebody asked. As Frau Wieth never did anything special, they pretty much left her out of the conversation, but when it was her turn, naive as she was, she said, "Ah, I had a wonderful evening yesterday. I had a lovely supper." "What did you have?" "Potato pancakes." "Potato pancakes?! Who made you potato pancakes?" She stood there and she didn't say, "I made them". She said, "Oh, my cleaner. She made me the potato pancakes. They were delicious." "They were delicious? You have to invite us for potato pancakes!"

She came home and told me this story. "You did what?" I asked. "Why did you have to tell them you had potato pancakes?" "Well, they asked me, so I told them." "And what are we going to do now?" "Ah," she said, "Don't worry." She always used to say, "Ah, don't worry." But I was worried. "What will you do? They want to come here and have potato pancakes!" "They will forget all about it," she said. "Well, I don't know if they'll forget all about it, because it is not something you have every day nowadays, potato pancakes," I said. The following day at work they asked her when they could come for potato pancakes. She came home and told me that. "So what are we going to do?" I asked again. "I don't know. They'll forget all about it." And with a gesture of her hand she dismissed the issue...

It went on like that for a number of days. Eventually I said, "You know what, Frau Wieth? We have to make potato pancakes, because it's going to get very suspicious. They will start asking why you don't invite them. You never invite anyone and they'll wonder." They all had some social lives, and she didn't. "We really have to make potato pancakes," I said. "Oh, how do you want to do that?" "We have to. Here's how we'll do it. I'll be making potato pancakes in the kitchen and you'll be coming and getting them, and bringing them to your colleagues." In those days it wasn't like it is today. Nowadays, when people come and sit at the table and then whenever a dish comes, it's, "I'll help you and take it to the kitchen when finished." It wasn't like that in those days; people who came to dinner sat down at the table and were served. And they never budged, never 'helped', *never* went to the kitchen. "I'll be making the pancakes in the kitchen with the door shut, you'll be coming, collecting them and bringing them to the table," I said. "That's it. That's how we'll do it. And you'll tell them that your maid is making the potato pancakes."

So the visitors came: a man and two women. They went

straight to the living room and sat at the table, while I was making the potato pancakes and Frau Wieth was coming and going. Nobody came to help, thank God. She was bringing the pancakes to the table about five or six at a time. Then they wanted tea with lemon. I made tea with lemon and she served the tea. And that was that. They were all over there, I was in the kitchen. It was all done. And then I heard some commotion. They were leaving. The entrance door to the apartment was very close by the kitchen. The kitchen was on the right and the room was on the left. I could hear them talking, saying their thank yous, and suddenly I heard the man's voice, "Oh, no, just a moment. I have to reward your maid for the potato pancakes." He was almost by the entrance door. When I heard that, I quickly hid in the scullery. Frau Wieth stood by the door. "No, no, no. Don't do that, no, no, no." "I have to. The pancakes were very nice. I must reward her. Please allow me to reward her." And Frau Wieth said, "No, she's terribly shy, she won't like it. And she doesn't speak German." He must have pushed her aside though. He opened the door and there was nobody in the kitchen. How did Frau Wieth not faint? I don't know! She stood there and there was nobody. She just said, "You see? I told you, she's really very shy. She must have left already. I never hear her when she comes or when she's leaving. She's so very quiet and shy, she doesn't speak any German. She must have gone home, she must have gone while we were sitting and having supper." The man said, "Never mind. Here, I put it on the table. When she comes tomorrow, thank her for us. The dinner was very nice. This money is for her."

Ever since then, every single time I have potato pancakes, I remember that scene. Every single time, until today. I hear him, the gentleman, saying, "But I must reward her, they were so delicious, they were so good, you must allow me..."

At some point you started sneaking out of the apartment?

Well, we had to eat. My mother joined us in May, when the ghetto was on fire, after my brave, wonderful grandmother committed suicide. This was a tragedy. My grandfather was already dead by that point. Grandmother jumped out of the third floor window, so that my mother would leave her and join me. But she didn't die on the spot. So my poor mother had to get an ambulance and a doctor. And at the same time, the ghetto was in flames... Max Kohl, the German owner of the factory where my mother worked, sent a doctor and an ambulance. She begged the doctor to free her mother from the pain. The doctor gave her an injection and promised she would suffer no more. My mother was by her mother's side. After my poor grandmother was gone, my mother escaped from the ghetto, took her armband off, and in a white day, full of fumes from the ghetto, she walked to the other side of the city again, to the SS and police district where Frau Wieth lived, to me... And nobody stopped my beautiful, brave mother, even though it was still daytime, not curfew. A miracle...

From then on there were four of us hiding in the flat. Frau Wieth liked my mother very much, but she was less fond of the other couple. She didn't show it, she did not make them feel uncomfortable. But whatever she had to discuss, it was always with my mother, my mother and me. She respected my mother greatly.

There were four of us and we had to eat, so I started going shopping. My mother made a *dirndl* for me and I looked like any other young German girl. I was out in the street and nobody even looked at me. I could have passed the Gestapo, the SS or soldiers, and they never gave me a second look. I was like one of them. Also by that time I spoke fluent German. But I was always very apprehensive about being spotted by somebody who might have known me from before. In other words by one of the locals, either Poles or Ukrainians. But I had to shop!

I was in the German part of the city, in the SS district. I was in the lion's den, but, paradoxically, it was probably the safest place to be. The shops were for Germans only, *nur für Deutsche*, nobody else could shop there, however those doing the shopping were usually maids, local maids, mostly Ukrainian maids employed by German families. So it wasn't very comfortable for me. Hence when I went into a shop, I never queued. I never wanted to give myself more time than was necessary, so I went straight to the counter. It was not very nice, but I had to do it. I went straight to the counter, jumping the queue, and *demanded* to be served. I said I didn't have time to spare and I needed this, this and this. And quickly! I always carried a leather folder with two photographs. These were photos of the man whose apartment we were in. They were a real lifesaver for me. On one side, there was a picture of him in the black SS officer's uniform and a cap with *Totenkopf,* and on the other one there was a picture of him without the cap, but still in the officer's uniform. I kept my money under the photographs in this folder. When paying, I would open the folder wide, so that everybody could see the two photographs. These photos were my documents, my ID. I had no other papers.

Now and again, I did hear comments from the women in the queue, "Look at her! Look at this Kraut girl! If one didn't know she was German, you would think she was a Jew." When I heard that, I quickly opened the folder, took the money out from under the clearly visible photographs, paid, and was out. That was that. Nobody batted an eyelid.

It was such a psychologically astute way of playing this situation to your advantage...

It certainly deserved five Oscars! Don't ask me how I did it. I don't know how, I don't know why. I don't think I would be able to do it today.

But did you act on instinct, at least at first, or did you think it through beforehand?

I often had this feeling that there was somebody behind my back, somebody looking at me. This certainly was an instinct. Many things were done *purely* on instinct. The fact was: I had to do it that way, I could not queue like everybody else. First of all, I was supposedly German, so why would I queue? The ones queuing were the maids. I decided to use my 'superiority', with audacity – not very polite – but that's how it had to be done every single time, there was no other way for *me* to shop.

Until one fine day in June. It was Frau Wieth's birthday and I thought, "Oh, my God, it's her birthday. What am I going to do? I have absolutely nothing to give her, nothing. I need a present!" There was a flower woman selling cut flowers on the corner on the opposite side of the street. So I thought, "I'm going to go down and get some flowers for her." I slipped downstairs, which at all times was easier said than done: three flights of stairs, not to be spotted by anyone, and I went across the street, got the flowers, paid, went back. I remember I got peonies and ever since then when I see a peony I remember 17 June 1943. I got her the peonies and she was truly thrilled. She said, "How did you get them?" And I told her. She wasn't too pleased I went out.

A few days later, she came back home from the office terribly flushed and upset, almost crying. I asked, "My God Almighty, what happened to you? Why are you like this? What's going on?" "Oh, it's terrible, so terrible," she was shaking. "When I walked into the building, the caretaker's wife was sitting on the stairs, crying, sobbing. So I asked her why she was crying, what happened to her. She said that the Gestapo came to them at night and were looking for a Jewish girl. They turned the whole place upside down. They told them that there was no Jewish girl at theirs, that they didn't know anything about any Jewish girl here, but they, the Gestapo, were insistent. They didn't find the Jewish girl, so they took her husband and now he is being tortured by the Gestapo."

It became obvious that it must have been I who was seen entering the building by somebody who knew me from before, and denounced me to the Gestapo. How else would they know? I looked like any other German child in that district, so why would they look for a Jewish girl? Typically, the Gestapo came in the middle of the night, and who do they go to? To the only ones not German, not SS, not Gestapo, not *Schutzpolizei,* not even the Ukrainian family below us. The Gestapo didn't go searching into any other apartment, but straight to the Polish caretaker's. Even today I have this terrible feeling of guilt inside me, when I think of that night. Here was an innocent man being subjected to torture. Eventually they let him go. But just imagine that poor woman, sitting and crying her eyes out, the whole place upside down? They didn't find anyone and were furious, so they took him away. When the Soviets came in 1944, I thought, "I must go there, to confront the caretaker, apologise to them. I must talk to these unfortunate people." I went, but they weren't there anymore. I don't know what happened to them. What I do know is that the Gestapo did let him go, and he came back home, but apparently after having suffered torture.

Did you ever bump into anybody who knew you from the past?

Yes, into this notoriously cruel Ukrainian policeman called Andruszko, whose name alone brought shivers down the spine. He didn't know me very well, we never spoke, but he did remember me from the past. He used to come to the building we lived in during the first Soviet occupation, to see his friend Stefan, our caretaker, the same caretaker who denounced my father. For Andruszko then, I was just a

Jewish child who played downstairs with other children from the building.

One day, I left Frau Wieth's and was going shopping. I went to a different shop than usually. Why I went there, I don't know. But while I was walking to the shop, I suddenly spotted him a mere few metres away from me. He was standing there with a smirk on his face, rubbing his hands... He found himself a victim, he had me. He was looking straight at me with this terrible smirk on his face. I recognised him instantly, and thought, "That's it. He knows me. I have no escape." I kept walking towards him, while a lot was going through my head. I was thinking, "What do I do? I can't run. If I start running, he will catch me easily. There is nothing I can do but walk on." And I kept walking, like I walked when the two soldiers stood guard outside the barracks near the ghetto. I was getting closer and closer to him. I can never say what made me do what I did, I have no idea.

Suddenly I stood in front of him and, in a very loud voice, said in German, "Please tell me where is the building called Organisation Todt?" Why I asked it, I shall never know, but I knew that there was such a building in the area. "Can you show me the way to this building?" I asked in German. And suddenly his hands went down, his smirk disappeared and he stood motionless. He was like a stone. I said, raising my voice, "Well? I'm asking you a question and you're not answering. I'm in a hurry! Where is that building?" He still didn't say anything. He stood there motionless, like a stone... I continued in a raised voice, "Can't you understand what I'm saying to you? How long have we been here? Two years, a year and a half? And you still don't understand what I'm saying?!" He didn't say a word, he was like a pillar of salt.

Meanwhile other people started gathering around us and somebody said, "I will show you the way. I know where that place is." It was some Polish man. I said, "Oh, thank you very much indeed. At least you understand what I'm saying. So where is it?" "Just around the corner, there. You know, this building there..." I thanked him and to the other one I said, almost shouting at him, "It's about time you understood what people say to you here." And I started walking away, as if nothing had happened. I walked slowly, but as soon as I was around the corner, I ran like a wild animal. I don't even remember where I ran. I left him completely aghast. Don't ask me what made me do what I did – I have no idea, not even today. Until I stopped in front of him, I didn't know what I was going to do. In fact, I could only think this was going to be my end.

You were to be his victim and you suddenly swapped places with him...

Exactly, I was to be his victim, in fact, he found himself a victim. He had me, and suddenly that twist of fate... He was completely stunned, he just stood there, flabbergasted, like a mummy. A moment ago he was rubbing his hands, now he stood almost to attention, incapable of understanding what was going on. And not a sound came out of him, not a sound. The longer he stayed silent, the more I raised my voice.

You had another quite incredible encounter with the Katzmann family...

I didn't know who they were. Sometimes when shopping I saw this woman with her children. I didn't pay them any attention. The only thing I wanted when out was to be done with shopping *quickly,* and to disappear. That was all. I didn't look around much. But on that particular occasion this German lady approached me and asked why I was shopping on my own. I was just a child, you see, not a usual sight. I said, "Well, because I have to." "Why?" "My mother is ill, so I'm doing the shopping." "Oh," she said, and then turned to the children, "Look, what a lovely little girl! Would you do that for me? Her mother is unwell, so she goes shopping to help her mother. How very nice!" She turned to me, "Would you like to come with us? We live nearby. Would you like to come and have some orangeade?" It was summer. "Oh, I don't know if I can," I said. "My mother would be very worried, you know. I told her I wouldn't be long." "Why don't you come just for a few minutes and then go home? You are such a nice girl." She seemed normal, there seemed to be nothing to fear, so I thought, "Well, maybe I just say yes to be polite, stay just for five minutes or so, and then go home." So I said yes and went with them.

Janowska concentration camp commandant Friedrich Warzok, SS-Gruppenfuhrer Fritz Katzmann, Reichsfuehrer SS Heinrich Himmler

It was a villa with a garden. The lady brought out some orangeade or some other cold drink. While we were drinking and talking, a uniformed SS-man walked in. I immediately recognised him. Oh my God! Children ran and kissed him, "Papi! Papi!" Normal scene, a father with his children. You would never know that this was a member of the SS, one whom we all feared[19]. He looked at me and said to his

---

[19] Fritz Katzmann (6 May 1906 – 19 September 1957) was a German SS and police official during the Nazi era. A major figure during the Holocaust, he perpetrated genocide in the cities of Katowice, Radom, Lemberg, Gdańsk, and across the Nazi German District of Galicia. In 1943, Katzmann wrote a top-secret report summarising Operation Reinhard in Galicia. The Katzmann Report is considered one of the most important pieces of evidence

children, "Ah, I see that you have a friend over?" "No, we met her while shopping. We don't know her." Then the mother added, "She's a nice girl. She was shopping and we asked her to come over and have a glass of orangeade. Her mother is not well, which is why she was shopping." I quickly said, "Yes, I better go. My mother is very unwell and she would be very worried." And his response was, "Oh, come, sit down for a bit." He shook my hand. "What's your name?" My name was always Lili. Lili was fine. So I said, "My name is Lili. But I really must go." I said my goodbyes and left. I never went there again. I never went to that same shop again.

It was terrible to see him walk in like this, his children running, calling "Papi! Papi!" And just a few months earlier there was a selection where we were all taken, the four of us. It was always between the *Schutzpolizei* and the Gestapo, they disliked each other. When the *Schutzpolizei* did something, then the Gestapo wanted to outdo them and vice versa. The *Schutzpolizei* took us in a large selection and the Gestapo wasn't keen on their operation. Suddenly, we heard, "Katzmann is coming. He is very angry, because things were done without his permission." My little brother and I managed to escape while he was about to enter. So now, to suddenly see this man walking in and his children running to welcome him, to see a father who kissed his children, the same man who was killing us…?! I stood next to him thinking that if he knew who I was, he would shoot

---

of the extermination process. He managed to escape prosecution after the war, living under a false identity.

me without hesitation. That was what was going through my head while he held my hand, "If he knew, he would shoot me on the spot, if only he knew…"

It's quite amazing that you kept a cool head in all those situations.

The situations *demanded* that. From one second to the next, what befell us there, we would not be possible to get out of today, we just wouldn't have the 'sixth sense' we had then… That time when I escaped with my little brother, my mother told us that they were dividing people into two groups, to the left and to the right. She said to me, "You have to take Uryś and escape." "I'm not going to do that, I'm not leaving here." She insisted, "You have to take the child, you have to take Uryś and run."

So when they were doing this 'left-right' selection, I took him and we ran away. There was a guard who, I'm sure, saw us, but he turned away. I'm sure he saw us, it was impossible not to see us. But we managed to get out. This was in March 1942, during the so-called 'great March selection'[20]. I immediately went to talk to somebody to help get my parents out. I needed some 'official' to intervene for them,

---

[20] The Lemberg Ghetto was one of the first to have Jews transported to the death camps as part of Operation Reinhard, the secretive German plan to exterminate Poland's Jews in the General Government district of German-occupied Poland. Between 16 March and 1 April 1942 approximately 15,000 Jews were taken to the Kleparów railway station and deported to the Bełżec extermination camp.

so I went to the *Judenrat*[21], to a man who was a lawyer friend from Kraków, and I pleaded, "You've got to help me, you've got to do something to get my parents out." He said, "Go home to my wife, my child. She's at home. Both of you stay there and I'll do what I can." And he did. At six o'clock in the morning my parents knocked at the door, he got them out.

What about that time when you bumped into someone who recognised Sepp, the man in the photos?

He recognised him from the photo I had in my folder when I was taking my money out. It was the only time I ever queued, because there were just two or three people in front of me outside the shop. One was already being served, the others were about to be served, so I thought that, for once, I wouldn't go straight to the counter, I would wait. Two or three people only, I could queue. So I'm queuing and suddenly somebody embraces me from behind, all excited, "It's Sepi! It's Sepp!" I was getting my money out to pay and get out of there as quickly as possible, and that's when this man spotted the photo. It was a horror. I had no idea who he was, but he obviously knew whose photo I had in my hands. He turned me around and said, "My God, you are a big girl now." So I realised that this man must have known

---

[21] *Judenrat* was a Second World War administrative agency imposed by Nazi Germany on Jewish communities across occupied Europe, principally within the ghettos, including those of German-occupied Poland. The Germans required Jews to form a *Judenrat* in every community across the occupied territories.

the family, must have known that Sepp had a daughter. "Where is your Papi? Where is he?" he asked, all excited. I said he was on the Eastern Front. "And your mum?" "At home, but she's not very well, so I need to do the shopping for her." "Oh, I want to see her. How are you all?" To which I said, "Well, I'll tell you all about it, but I have to do my shopping first. I'll wait for you outside while you shop." And while he was shopping, I ran, oh, how I run. I have no idea who this man was, no idea.

Earlier you mentioned Max Kohl, who helped your mother after your grandmother's failed suicide attempt. Your mother worked for him. What was he like?

He was a wonderful man, a 'mini Schindler'. Well, not so mini... Max Kohl, a German, did exactly the same thing – protected the Jewish people who were working for him. He employed about forty of them in his factory. He was a very well-known, pre-war leather tanner. He received many prizes, world prizes, for his skins, and not just in Germany. He was a well-known expert in his field. I think first he was in Lublin or Białystok, and then they brought him to Lemberg, and wanted him to open a factory to make coats for the Gestapo, those famous black leather coats. He said, "All right, I'll open a factory, but only in the ghetto." They didn't want to agree, so he said, "Then there will be no factory," and he left.

Eventually they brought him to Lemberg again and this time allowed him to open a factory in the ghetto. They asked him "Why do you want it in the ghetto?" "Do you want to have beautifully done coats?" he replied. "The Jews are the best artisans and I don't want my leather done by just anybody, I want them done by the people who know how to do a beautiful coat. If you want it done beautifully, then that's what I want."

When my mother went from Frau Wieth's back to the ghetto, she needed to be employed. And Max Kohl was a friend of Frau Wieth's, so she asked him and he took my mother in. He looked after his Jewish workmen in the best way he could. On more than one occasion the Gestapo came to take them away, but he refused to let them go. He took bales of the best leather under his arm and went to the Gestapo, to bribe whoever needed to be bribed. And he kept bribing them in this way, so that they would leave his people be. Until the moment came when he could do no more for his people…

So after the fire in the ghetto, and after your grandparents both had perished, your mother joined you in Frau Wieth's apartment and then there were four of you hiding there. Was it crowded? Did you quarrel?

No, nobody quarrelled. The four of us slept on the floor in the kitchen. It was crowded, it wasn't a big apartment. We were not supposed to move during the day. We were all in the kitchen, cooped up, couldn't walk, couldn't do anything. Every morning the other three – my mother and Mr and Mrs Podoszyn – were waiting for me to wake up. Why? They didn't want me to forget my dream. "So, tell us, tell us quickly what happened today? What happened in your dream? What happened?" I had a recurring dream, not every night, but now and again. And they didn't want to miss the next instalment. I dreamt that I was at a peace conference with Stalin, Churchill, Hitler and Roosevelt... And I was translating for them from one language to another. At the time I didn't know any of the languages at all, other than German and some Russian, and yet I was translating between English, Russian and German. That was my recurring dream. Until today I can't understand how it was possible. How is it possible that in a dream you can speak any language, while in reality – not a word? I would also dream that I was reciting poems. No idea what any of the poems were. I didn't know a poem like this, and I had never read it, I had never heard it. In my dream I just stood there, reciting it. I don't even know whether it was in Polish, or in some other language. At that time I didn't even speak much German yet. Apart from Polish, I only knew Russian, but in the dream I was translating for Stalin, for Roosevelt, and for Churchill.

At some point while we were with her, Frau Wieth had a short liaison with an army officer. He was a major in the *Wehrmacht*, a pharmacist by profession, a cultured, couth, educated person. He came once a week, on a Wednesday, and stayed until Thursday morning. And then he was gone until next Wednesday. To us he didn't represent danger, because, as I said before, in those days it wasn't done for a visitor to come to the kitchen. Frau Wieth did, but not a visitor, and so he came and went, but never even came near the kitchen.

One day he gave her an ultimatum, "It's either the garlic

or me!" I did not mention it before, but Frau Wieth was a great advocate of garlic, and would consume it every single day. She was obsessed with it, believing that no doctors were needed if you consumed it, that it was the best medicine. "Look, I can't take this anymore," he added. "So which is it going to be, the garlic or me?" She replied, "Sorry, if I have to make this choice, it's the garlic." So, off he went and never came back.

She needed no social life. Garlic was paramount! It, undoubtedly, was a contributory factor to saving our lives. I prepared a whole head of it for her daily!

Then one fine memorable morning arrived. It was a Thursday, about six o'clock. To say that we were sleeping is saying too much. We slept, but always remained very alert. On that particular morning, I suddenly heard some noise by the entrance door, like scraping of a key in the lock. It was very quiet, I didn't hear anybody's steps, didn't hear the lift, but definitely heard a key in the lock. I immediately alerted the others, "Something is going on. Wake up. Wake up!"

We instantly got hold of our so-called 'bedding', went into the scullery and locked ourselves inside. We could hear screaming and shouting in German, "Open up! Open up!" A man was shouting at the top of his voice. It was six o'clock in the morning. He couldn't get in, because the door was on a chain, and so he got more and more furious and screamed at the top of his voice, "Open up! Open up!" We were petrified. Was it the Gestapo? Frau Wieth, on the other hand, knew this voice. Who else could have the key to the apartment? So, shakingly, she opened the door. It was Sepp, the owner of the apartment. We were in a state. The four of us were in the tiny scullery, where there was barely enough space for two, and hardly any air... We were locked in there, so when Frau Wieth looked into the kitchen, she saw nobody there. On opening the entrance door, she said, "Why are you screaming?" He started running like a man possessed, shooting all over the place, screaming obscenities. "Where is he, this so-and-so of yours?" Obscene language. He was shooting all over the place, into the bed, under the bed, into the wardrobe, there was shooting, shooting... It was an absolute horror!

She ran out onto the balcony. She always used to say, "I'm not going to fall into the hands of the Gestapo, never!" So she went out on the balcony and – she told us afterwards – should he run into the kitchen, should she hear four shots, she would jump. Finally he came running into the kitchen. Nobody there. He stood in front of the scullery door. Our hearts were beating so hard that you could probably hear them from as far as in the hallway! And, too late, we realised that the key was inside the door! We didn't think when we locked ourselves in. He tried the handle to open the door, banged on it, then turned around and went away. He didn't shoot, even though the door was locked. Had he looked inside the lock, that would have been the end of us, as the key was still on the inside! But he left. Of all the places he did not shoot at, the scullery! And how did he not hear our heartbeats?! A miracle.

He found Frau Wieth and asked, "What are you doing on the balcony?" "Well, you were shooting all over the place, so I went out of the way. I don't want to be shot by you." "So where is he?" "I don't know what you mean.

Who? What? I don't know why you're shouting and I don't know who you mean, I don't know!" What happened was that a 'good' friend of hers, who knew them both from before, corresponded with him while he was away. And she told him, "While you are away, she's having a very nice time. She has found herself somebody else!" And Sepp, being as obsessed as he was, decided that he was going to come unbeknown to her, and catch them *in flagrante* on a Thursday morning.

And he did arrive on a Thursday morning. He said, "A friend wrote to me and she told me…" Frau Wieth replied, "Well, I don't know who wrote to you and what she wrote to you about, but, as you can see, there is nobody here." "Oh, well," he said, "in this case I'm going to stay. I have a furlough, I took two weeks off. I will just go to get my luggage. I left it at the station. I'll be back." And off he went to get the luggage. Imagine the situation!

Frau Wieth came to the kitchen. All of us were in quite a state. "What am I going to do with you now?" she said. "What am I going to do with you?" Even my mother, who was a very wise person and never panicked, said, "He'll be back very soon. We have to think quickly." They decided that two out of the four of us would stay in the kitchen, my mother and the other lady, Mrs Podoszyn. Mrs Podoszyn was to play the role of Frau Wieth's housekeeper, or a maid, doing cooking and cleaning. And my mother was to be her dressmaker, since Frau Wieth was allowed to have one. The two of us – Mr Podoszyn and I – were to hide in the scullery. My mother said, "I'm going to put a table against the scullery door and the two of us will pretend to be Ukrainians. We will not understand or speak any German. If he talks to us we just say, '*Nichts verstehen.*'" And that's how it was.

He came back with his luggage and stayed for two weeks. We remained in hiding, while my mother was in the kitchen, sewing, and the other lady was cooking and cleaning. Frau Wieth had to go to work, so Sepp had too much time on his hands. Bored, he would come into the kitchen and talk incessantly. He talked and talked, and was telling my mother and Mrs Podoszyn about the Nazis progressing on all fronts, about Germany winning the war in Africa and in Russia, on all fronts. My mother was worried that I might burst out laughing, because sometimes what he was saying was so absurd that it was quite funny. There he was, sitting down, wanting to know, "How are you cooking this or that? Show me." He was a 'home lover', he liked to stay in, and so he didn't go anywhere, just sat in the kitchen all the time. With four Jews.

Poor Frau Wieth had to entertain Sepp non-stop, so that he wouldn't even think about grabbing a glass of water for himself. She told him, "Look, you are on holiday, you've been working very hard. I want you to rest. Let me do things for you."

I don't know if she was aware of what he was responsible for. I don't imagine he told her. He was an SS Obersturmbahnführer, at the time the commandant of a concentration camp in the Netherlands. She would bring him food, she would have water by his side of the bed, so he didn't need to go to the kitchen. One night she said to him, "Look, it's going to be better if the maid and the seamstress sleep here, instead of going home. It's late, there is curfew.

They sometimes sleep here. They'll stay in the kitchen and sleep on the floor, so don't go there, because they would be very embarrassed if you did. Whatever you need, tell me and I'll go get it for you." And that's how it was for two weeks. What she did was *heroic*. Every day she went to work and never knew what she would find coming back. Can you imagine how *brave* she was?

At night Mr Podoszyn and I would come out of the scullery and all four of us slept on the floor in the kitchen. I don't remember what we did when we needed to go to the toilet. Maybe we didn't need to go? I don't know. My mother and Mrs Podoszyn could go if they needed, because they were outside, but we, in the scullery, we couldn't. Not even at night.

Even after the war, and until the end of her days, Sepp's name was never mentioned.

We only talked about this whole situation once. I remember we were in Israel, staying with friends, and Frau Wieth and I shared a room. We were chatting before going to bed and she asked me, "Tell me, Lili, did that really happen? Did he come and was there for two weeks? Did it really happen?" "Yes, it happened. Yes. And we pulled it off. *You* pulled it off!" A miracle…

Lili's grandmother on her mother's side, Hinda Brück

Historical Context
19 November 1942 – November 1943
Clare Mulley

By late 1942, hundreds of thousands of Jews from across Europe had been sent to Nazi concentration camps. Among these were 60,000 from the Netherlands, where the owner of the Frau Wieth's apartment, SS officer Sepp, was a camp commandant. The following year, mass murders started in the Auschwitz gas chambers. Over a million people would be murdered at this site alone during the war.

On the day that Lili gave Frau Wieth birthday peonies, the Germans sank a British troopship off Libya, killing all on board, yet by now the Third Reich was also suffering severe setbacks. Allied victory at El Alamein in North Africa had opened up a second front and, at Casablanca, Churchill and Roosevelt began discussing a cross-channel invasion.

By June 1943 the British and American Air Forces were bombing Germany. Meanwhile, having hoisted a Soviet flag over recaptured Stalingrad in February, the Red Army had turned the tide of the war on the Eastern Front.

CHAPTER FOUR
ARCHBISHOP METROPOLITAN SHEPTYTSKY. LIBERATED LVOV

November 1943 – July 1945

*

Anna Blasiak: Like pretty much everybody else around me in Poland in the 1970s and 1980s, I am raised as a Catholic. I go to school and, on top of school, to religious classes at the church. Every church has the special classrooms built next to it. Every church runs religious classes. Every Polish child attends them. Or so I think.

Even though at school I learn a little bit about followers of other faiths in Poland of the past, I never see them, I don't meet them in the streets. With one small exception. This exception is St Hyacinth Church in Słupsk which happens to be the church I choose to attend as a teenager, when I go through my last attempt at finding a place for myself within the Catholic institution. St Hyacinth was built for the Dominicans at the turn of the thirteenth and fourteenth centuries, then used by Lutherans and Calvinists from the sixteenth century onwards, to then go back into the hands of the Catholics after the Second World War. But in my days, in the 1980s, there is also a weekly service in St Hyacinth attended by the Greek Catholic community. That continued until they built their own church in Słupsk in 2004.

Only much later I learn that there were also Jewish

133

settlers in Słupsk, as early as in the beginning of the eighteenth century. In 1874, a hundred years before I was born, there are nearly 900 Jewish citizens of Słupsk. Growing up I never hear about them and never see any physical remnants of their presence.

Catholicism disappoints me and I start rebelling against it. Very quickly I develop a stronger and stronger yearning for a completely different world. I start dreaming about a country, a place under the sun, where people of different beliefs live in peace side by side, where religion, any religion, can blend into the background, instead of being the deciding factor, the main mould of social and political lives. Where religion, if practiced at all, is only practiced in private, to the point of becoming invisible. Where it doesn't matter what your religion is, if any at all. But achieving this kind of world is tricky. And one of the ways of getting there is building bridges, learning to understand other religions, sometimes perhaps even crossing over. I think of those who managed to do it successfully...

One of them was Andrey Sheptytsky (Szeptycki) who was born Roman Aleksander in 1865 in the family of polonized Roman Catholic aristocrats in their estate in Prylbychi in the eastern part of the Kingdom of Galicia and Lodomeria, then a crownland of the Austrian Empire, now – Ukraine. His mother, Aleksandra, was the daughter of Aleksander Fredro, a well-known Polish poet and playwright whose works every Polish child reads every Polish child reads as part of the school curriculum. Roman Aleksander was one of seven brothers, the eldest of the five who survived beyond childhood. He was always deeply entrenched in Polish culture and loved Polish language and literature. After studying law in Wrocław and Kraków, he travelled to Rome in 1886 and was granted an audience with Pope Leo XIII in the Vatican. This was the time of the growing crisis within the Ukrainian Greek Catholic Church and there were stronger and stronger leanings to unite with the Eastern Orthodox Church in Russia. Sheptytsky was seeking support from the Pope for his ideas for keeping the Ruthenians within the Catholic faith. Two years later, despite his father's opposition, young Roman Aleksander decided to leave the Roman Catholic Church and join the Greek Catholic Church. He became a monk in the Basilian Monastery in Dobromyl. He took the name Andrey. At the age of 34 he was appointed Ukrainian Greek Catholic Bishop of Stanislau, a year later – Metropolitan Archbishop of Lemberg. All his life he worked towards peaceful relations between Ukrainian and Polish nations in Galicia. He travelled extensively, including to the United States and Canada, where he met with Ukrainian immigrant communities.

At the outbreak of the First World War, Sheptytsky was arrested by the Russians and imprisoned in a monastery. Upon his release in 1918, he returned to Lwów. Bolsheviks destroyed his family estate in Prylbychi. Lost were also the family archives.

During the First World War he went through scarlet fever, as a result of which he developed rheumatoid arthritis which impeded his movements. First he used crutches, but eventually ended up in a wheelchair. He could only write with his left hand.

As a student, he learned Hebrew in order to relate better to Jewish communities in Ukrainian villages which he visited. During the Second World War, from the very beginning of the Nazi occupation, he provided a safe haven for hundreds of Jewish people in his own residence and in Greek Catholic monasteries and convents. He set up a network of help for the Jews together with his brother, Klymentiy Sheptytsky, who also converted and became a Greek Catholic monk. They created orphanages especially to provide hiding places for Jewish children, a boys' one by the Studite Brethren monastery in Univ near Peremyshliany, as well as two girls' ones, in Yaktoriv near Peremyshliany and in Lemberg itself. There was also a nursery for babies that monks or nuns managed to smuggle out of the ghetto. Adults with 'good looks' were given Aryan papers. Some were also hidden in convents and monasteries. Pretty much all of the Studite monasteries and convents were providing safe havens to the Jews. Nearly 500 monks and nuns knew about this operation, but not a word ever got out. Not one person taken by the Greek Catholics into their care and protection died.

Sheptytsky called himself the 'friend of the Jews'. He openly spoke in defence of the persecuted Jews, criticised Nazi atrocities, strongly forbade the Ukrainian faithful of his church from participating or helping the Germans to kill the Jews when no other leader of any church did the same. He also issued secret instructions to his secular and monastic clergy in which he ordered them to help the Jews by hiding them on church property, feeding them or smuggling them out of the country. In the first days of the pogroms he sent *his priests out to town to control the Ukrainian mob attacking the Jews. He sent an official letter to Hitler and Himmler protesting about the destruction of the Jews. Israeli daily 'Haaretz' called Sheptytsky the 'Ukrainian Schindler'. People saved by him, including Lili Pohlmann, tried on several occasions to get him the title of the Righteous Among the Nations, so far unsuccessfully, mainly because of his initial belief that German invaders would be better for Ukraine than the atrocious Soviet Union had been.*

In 1958 the cause for his canonisation began. In 2015 Pope Francis proclaimed Sheptytski to be Venerable.

He was a pioneer of ecumenism. He strove for reconciliation between different ethnic groups and wrote on social issues and spirituality. His tenure spanned two world wars and seven political regimes: Austrian, Russian, Ukrainian, Polish, Soviet, General Government (Nazi), and again Soviet.

Sheptytsky died in November 1944.

Metropolitan Andrey Sheptytsky

*

Anna Blasiak: Frau Wieth was evacuated back to Germany when the Soviets were approaching...

Lili Pohlmann: Twice there were rumours about the Germans being evacuated, but the first time nothing happened, because the Soviet army retreated. But then, in November 1943, the rumours spread again. Frau Wieth called us for a meeting and told us that she was being evacuated back to Germany. She had to go. "What am I going to do with you?" those were her words. To which Mr Podoszyn said, "Well, you don't need to worry about me and my wife. We have somewhere we can go." "Oh, really?" she said. "That's wonderful. So where are you going to go?" He explained. "Okay, that's very nice," she said, and then she turned to my mother, "And you, Frau Stern? Do you have somewhere to go with Lili?" My mother said that no, we didn't, but Frau Wieth should not worry about that, she should do as she was told. "Whatever happens, happens. We might find somewhere." So Frau Wieth said to Mr Podoszyn, "Right, I want you to know that either *all* of you go or nobody goes. If you have somewhere to go, you better arrange for Lili and her mother to come as well. Don't you forget why you are here. Look at this girl. You and your wife are here thanks to her. So you better do as I tell you. If not, *nobody* goes."

That was what she was like, honourable, downright decent, upright. Her principles were principles... "Well, I don't know how...," he said and then added, "Never mind. I have cyanide, so my wife and I can take it." "Oh, is that what you have?"Frau Wieth said. "How very interesting.

141

Show me what it looks like." So he brought out two little ampules and said, "This is it, for me and my wife." And Frau Wieth said, "Well, you better get hold of four of them. If you only have two, you won't get them back. I won't give them back to you. Either everybody or nobody."

Long before the war Mr Podoszyn was the manager of a very well-known pharmacy in Lwów, and they were delivering medicines to the church, the Greek Catholic Ukrainian church, and its Metropolitan Archbishop Andrey Count Sheptytsky. Somehow Mr Podoszyn had arranged with the Metropolitan that if anything were to happen, Sheptytsky would take him and his wife. Their son, who was about my age, was already in one of the monasteries[22]. The plan was for them to go to St. George's Cathedral. And he arranged the same for my mother and me too.

The story goes that after the August 1942 selection, in which my father and my little brother died, the well-known Rabbi, Dr Lewin, who was also a personal friend of the Metropolitan, came to him asking for help to save Jewish people from death. Apparently the Metropolitan said, "I can take you and your family, but I can't take everybody." To which the Rabbi Lewin replied, "Well, I didn't come to plea for my family and for myself, I came to plea for my people. If you can't do it, I am sorry." At this point Ukrainian police

---

[22] At some point seven-year-old Ludwik Podoszyn was in care of Father Ivanyuk, who placed the boy with his parents in the countryside. Rumours spread locally that Ludwik might be Father Ivanyuk's illegitimate child. Ivanyuk was summoned by the diocese bishop and severely punished. He never denied it, not wanting to put the boy in danger.

was waiting for him outside his house. He was taken to the infamous Brygidki prison where he was tortured to death. From that moment on, the Metropolitan promised that whoever were to come to him, he would give them haven, take them in.

The Podoszyns went first and we followed the next day. Frau Wieth took us there. She said, "I want to see you on the other side, in the cathedral, otherwise I'm not going." We walked under the darkness of night, in deep snow and freezing temperature. As we went through the huge gates, it was late, and I can still see her standing there, in front of the gate, making sure that we made it safely to the other side, and were about to enter the Palace, the residence of the Metropolitan. We waved to her, tears flowing, and we were in.

A monk opened the gate for us and brought us in. The man wearing monk's clothes was Kurt Lewin, the son of the murdered Rabbi Lewin. Kurt was also in hiding, together with his brother Nathan, who was later sent to the monastery outside Lemberg. I didn't know who he was then. He told me years later that it was he who brought us into the Metropolitan's magnificent library and, apparently, I went under a table. I hid myself there, although I don't remember why, or any of this. Was I scared or embarrassed? I don't know. Even years later, Rabbi Lewin's son was saying, "I had to drag Lili out from under the table." We were asked to sit down and wait. The surroundings were amazing. After all it was a palace… Finally the door opened and they wheeled Metropolitan Sheptytsky in. He was in an invalid chair. They wheeled in this huge man, huge even in the sitting position, with leonine hair, a white mane. He looked like a saint, or like Wernyhora[23]. White beard, white, amazing hair and incredibly beautiful, blue eyes, the sort that can look right through you. Maybe that's what frightened me? He turned to my mother. He spoke Polish with her, because she couldn't speak Ukrainian. They discussed something and then he beckoned to me, so I came closer. I was frightened of him, I don't know why, but he had such an incredible presence! He was like no-one I had ever met. He asked me to come a little closer and he stroked me. He stroked my hair very gently and said to me in Ukrainian, "Don't be afraid, my child, no harm will come to you here." And I stopped feeling frightened *instantly*. As if somebody poured balsam over me, all my fears just went. And then he said, "Don't be afraid. You're going to stay here tonight, and tomorrow I'll send you to a very nice place, to a convent. I cannot keep everybody here. It would not be good, it would not be advisable." He turned to my mother. "Tomorrow morning you will go with Lili, and you will be staying with this very wonderful sister, who will look after you. She's our best. She is the Mother Superior Yosifa[24]. She will have you in her quarters. And Lili will be next door, in the orphanage." He stroked my hair again and was wheeled off...

---

[23] Wernyhora, a legendary 18th century Cossack bard who prophetized the fall of Poland and its subsequent rebirth and flourishing.

[24] Sister Ihumena Yosifa (Olena Viter) was the superior of the Studite convent in Lvov. In June 1940 she was imprisoned and tortured in order to 'confess' that Sheptytsky was a member of the Organization of Ukrainian Nationalists and that she was supplying him with weapons. She refused to do so.

How often did you see your mother? She was next door...

Yes, it was nearby. Mother Superior had her little house. It wasn't a palace like that of Sheptytsky's. She kept my mother with her, and, because my mother spoke no Ukrainian, she was to pretend to be deaf and dumb. How difficult was that? She kept her there out of sight, and out of fear. One feared one's own people...

We were far away from anywhere, on the outskirts of Lemberg. Soldiers didn't bother coming there. It was almost like a humble village: mud, no streets, no pavements. The very first evening when they brought me to the convent, it was supper time and one of the nuns introduced me to the other children. Everybody was staring at me. Of course, somebody new arrived, so they were all looking. And the nun told them my name and said, "She's your new friend." Everybody sat down and we started eating. After dinner there were prayers and then we were to go to bed. So we stood up for the prayers and, of course, I was trying to do what the others were doing.

As I stood up I saw a friend. We went to school together at the time of the Soviets, the first time they occupied Lvov. She was Jewish, like myself, but, contrary to myself, she was blonde and blue-eyed. She was looking at me, I was looking at her, and I could see she was afraid, afraid of me! We were both not so much scared of each other, as trying not to show that we knew each other... It was a terrible feeling. I don't know why. We were looking, but we pretended not to know each other.

There were prayers and everybody crossed themselves. Being Greek Catholics, they crossed themselves three times, from right to left, but what did I know? I crossed myself the only way I knew how, left to right, and only once. Children were looking at me anyway, because I was new, so they immediately spotted it. The nun, the one who brought me in and knew who I was, immediately said, "Why are you looking at Lidka?" That's what they called me there. "Lidka is half-Polish, her father was Polish, her mother Ukrainian, and she doesn't speak Ukrainian very well, because she was brought up speaking Polish. There are things she doesn't know, like crossing herself the way we do. She's here now, because her mother wants her to be with you." All right, fine, no problem. We were getting ready to go to bed and this nun said, "It's going to be hard, because we don't have a bed for you yet. It'll arrive tomorrow. You may have to sleep with somebody else." So the other Jewish girl *immediately* raised her hand. "I'll take her." And suddenly we were together in her bed. She told me to be quiet and then advised me about the situation there. She said, "We don't know each other, all right? We don't know each other at all. My name here is so-and-so." She told me all this while I was getting undressed. I was always half-decently dressed, never in some rags, like other impoverished children. My mother was able to make something for me out of nearly nothing. And while I was putting a nightgown on, I heard other girls saying "Look, look at her. Such a princess." All because I had a nightdress, while the other children had none. "Look at her, look at her in her nightie!"

After a while the situation settled and it was alright. We had nothing to complain about, the nuns were marvellous. I'm aware of maybe one or two of them who knew about us, but whether the others did, I don't know.

I had no papers, no documents whatsoever, which was not

a good thing. Everyone had an identity document, and I had nothing. So the Mother Superior, a very wonderful, very wise and kind woman, decided that I needed to get some identity papers. But how? And where from? There were some external, end-of-school exams going on in the city. If you wanted to get into a school, and if you passed the required exam, you could go to your chosen school. So, in her wisdom, she found out where the exams were taking place, and decided that I should go and sit this exam. In horror, I said, "How can I sit an exam? I have no knowledge about anything. And anyway, it's *dangerous!* Somebody might recognise me." "You will go with Sister Anastasia, she will take you there. And the minute you finish, you won't linger. You will both come straight back here. It will be fine." There were maybe a hundred children there and a number of teachers and examiners.

One of them I recognised, but he didn't recognise me. There were so many children… But I knew him, he was one of the school inspectors during the first Russian occupation. Once or twice, he came to my school and into my classroom. He sat there and witnessed a lesson. And now he was one of the examiners at my exam… I got so scared, but he obviously did not pay any attention to me. I was called to come forward. It was Ukrainian language. By that time I could speak it quite well. One of the teachers invited me to come closer, "What are you going to tell us? Can you recite anything? Can you tell us what you have read? Do you read sometimes?" "Yes, I read and I can recite. I'll recite Shevchenko[25]." The examiner seemed

---

[25] Taras Hryhorovych Shevchenko (9 March 1814 – 10 March 1861) was a Ukrainian poet, writer, artist, public and political

satisfied. Luckily, I always liked literature. I started reciting in Ukrainian of course, and the teacher said, "That's enough, that's fine, that's very nice. Go, sit down now." And I got a very good mark. The children there were mostly peasant children, with no education whatsoever, and suddenly there was I, a child who could recite Shevchenko. They all looked up. Next was mathematics. I was completely at a loss. What to do? But Mother Superior told me, "Look, it doesn't matter. Even if you get zero, even if you get the worst mark ever, you'll still have a piece of paper with your name on it." I remembered her words and I thought, "If I don't know, then I don't know. It doesn't matter." At the maths exam I was asked to draw a circle on the board, and then to halve it. "Which is the larger half?" I stood there speechless. I looked at the teacher and said, "There is no larger half." "What do you mean, there is no larger half?" "No, if it is a half, it is a half." And they were amazed. They gave me a good mark and told me to sit down. And I got my piece of paper with my name on it. It said, "Very good in Ukrainian, very good in maths." And it had my name on it!

I and the other girl in my group were *not* the only Jews Sheptytski and his clergy helped. He saved one hundred and fifty Jewish lives, primarily young children, but also grown-ups, girls and boys, which was particularly dangerous. They were hidden in monasteries, girls in convents. It was very dangerous. I was in one of them, in Ubocz, the only one I knew about. I had no idea about the others… I knew about that one girl, my

figure, as well as folklorist and ethnographer. His literary heritage is regarded to be the foundation of modern Ukrainian literature and, to a large extent, the modern Ukrainian language. Shevchenko is also known for many masterpieces as a painter and an illustrator.

former school friend, but I didn't know that there were other Jewish girls with us. I learned about it all later, much later....

The war for you ended in July 1944, but you did stay in Lvov for a bit longer, looking for some traces of your father and brother.

Yes, but there was nowhere to look. There were very few of us still there, about eighty people survived, that's all! And nobody knew anything. We were pretending to be non-Jews, my mother and I, we were still under assumed names, so it wasn't easy, but we kept trying, looking, asking, enquiring everywhere, wherever we could. We tried to establish something, but there was nothing. Silence... Eerie silence everywhere...

Lili Stern and Zosia Nacht, both kept in hiding in an orphanage thanks to Metropolitan Andrey Sheptytsky

Lili was isolated from events at the Greek Catholic convent that harboured her during the last years of the war. Had she known of the Battle of Monte Cassino in Italy in the spring of 1944, she could have felt proud of the decisive Polish contribution, while news of D-Day, on 6 June, marking the start of the Allied liberation of Europe, might have brought hope.

Sensing defeat, on 20 July 1944 some senior Wehrmacht officers undertook the most famous attempt on Hitler's life, although without success. Paris was liberated one month later, in August, Brussels soon after.

The Soviet offensive in Eastern Europe was now gathering pace. The Red Army retook Lemberg that summer, but chose to stop short of supporting the Warsaw Uprising. The ruined capital was a small price for them to pay for the decimation of Polish resistance.

The post-war fate of Europe was agreed between Churchill, Roosevelt and Stalin at the Yalta Conference in February 1945. Within two months, the combined strength of the Allied Armed Forces had secured a hard-won victory in Europe. Hitler committed suicide in his Berlin bunker on 7 May and the Nazi regime surrendered unconditionally.

The Holocaust had taken the lives of around six million Jews, almost half of whom had been Polish. While Britain, America and much of liberated Europe celebrated peace, Poland was among those Allies left in uncertainty about their future.

CHAPTER FIVE
KRAKÓW. RABBI SOLOMON SCHONFELD. LONDON
July 1945 – 1952

*

Anna Blasiak: I arrive in London for the first time in summer 1993, long before Poland joins the EU. I celebrate my last teen birthday with my new friends, Jane and Charles, who generously take me under their hospitable roof in Ladbroke Grove. I travel to the UK by ferry from Denmark, from Esbjerg, arriving in Harwich after a night on the boat's bunkbed in a shared sleeping quarters. The corridor leading to passport and immigration control is divided into two lanes. I am the first person off the boat, walking down the lane labelled 'Other Passports'. Everybody else is walking on the left, this is a lane for British/EU citizens. I feel very lonely in the right lane, I feel different, but I don't for a moment feel scared…

At immigration I have to show letters from my friends in London, Jane and Charles, stating clearly that they will provide accommodation and boarding for me while I'm in London. But the officer still wants to know how much money I have on me. At that time I don't own a credit card, I don't even have a bank account. But I do carry some cash, some pound sterling that my parents put aside at a considerable effort, so that I could go to London to practise my English. The officer asks me about my plans for the future (at that point I just passed my end of high school exams and was accepted at university. I am to start this same autumn). He also wants to know what my parents and grandparents do.

After a train journey from Harwich, I arrive at Victoria station in London. I follow my map, a folding paper map, and, for some reason, I decide that a tube journey to Ladbroke Grove and then a walk is a better idea than a bus ride. Even though the 52 bus starts right there, at the Bus Terminus in front of Victoria, and it would take me all the way to Jane's and Charles'. Next year I will correct this mistake and happily jump onto the number 52 bus.

Lili Pohlmann first arrived in London when she was just a little younger than I had been. The ship carrying her and other Jewish children brought to England as part of the first post-war Children's Transport organised by Rabbi Doctor Salomon Schonfeld, went under the Tower Bridge and let its passengers off on the very day when Lili turned sixteen. Already at this stage she spoke quite a few languages, but English wasn't one of them. That soon changed. When I come, I speak pretty good English, but – since a language is an identity – I still go through a proper culture shock and barely open my mouth for the first few weeks in London for fear of making the most terrible of mistakes. Lili must have struggled with this new world too, with the world so different to what she had left behind, with this new city. On the other hand she is and was a city person and she adapted quickly. London was her third city, after Kraków and Lwów, and was followed later by New York.

My friend Charles tests me by playing comedy

programmes on the radio when we are washing up after dinner. He watches my reactions. Good, I'm laughing when I should, he tells me. Lili's tests come in different forms, considerably more scary, at least some of them, for example being taken to the police station for explanations and thinking she was being deported.

Lili's English benefactor – a match for my Jane and Charles – was the man who brought her over, Rabbi Schonfeld. It was thanks to him that she managed to find this safe haven for herself, as well as for her mother and, eventually, for Frau Wieth.

Rabbi Doctor Solomon Schonfeld was a maverick Jewish leader who saved thousands of people from Nazi death camps, yet remains one of the least known Holocaust heroes. Before the war he ran the Children's Transport operation, as well as other rescue missions that helped many persecuted Jews escape Nazi Germany. After the war he helped many survivors of the concentration camps, including children. His service was only recognised by the British state in 2013, nearly 30 years after his death, when, on his behalf, his son was presented with a British Hero of the Holocaust award.

Rabbi Schonfeld was born in 1912. In 1933, at the age of only 21, he was already the head of an Orthodox Jewish community in north London and succeeded his father, Dr Avigdor Schonfeld, the founder of the Jewish Secondary Schools Movement, as principal of the Movement. When the Nazis came into power that same year, he immediately realised that Jews would have to leave Germany because of growing oppression and discrimination. He decided that elderly people and scholars should be his priority, since the younger and fitter people could try finding their way to Palestine. So he went to the Home Office and managed to secure five hundred visas for rabbis and their families to come to the United Kingdom. Altogether he organised a safe passage for some 1300 people. After Kristallnacht he brought further five hundred children and adults to the UK.

After the war, in 1946, he travelled with a convoy of lorries to Auschwitz and Bergen-Belsen concentration camps in an attempt to reach and help the survivors. He also organised more Children's Transports to bring Jewish children over to the UK. Of which Lili Pohlmann was one...

Altogether Rabbi Schonfeld has helped over 3500 people escape the persecutions in Central and Eastern Europe. Tens of thousands of people living in the UK now are only here because he saved their parents and grandparents.

*Jewish children and teenagers from Poland after arriving in
London in March 1946; Lili Stern third from the right*

Lili Pohlmann: It was a seven-day-long journey from Lvov to Kraków in summer 1945. It was fun for me, I quite enjoyed it, because there were many young people on the train. Not necessarily Jews, just youngsters. The train was full to capacity and it was incredibly hot. So we, the youngsters, climbed up to the roof of the train. My mother had a go at me, because I was one of those who climbed up... But there was no space to sit in the compartment. These would be difficult seven days to stay inside, so being on the roof was much better. And more fun, too. You know what youngsters are like!

We got to Kraków, and it was so terribly sad. We never went anywhere near the streets where we lived before the war. We had to find somewhere to live and my mother started working. She was designing and sewing again. So brilliant was she at it, that more and more people heard about her by word of mouth, and she could make a living. There was no school for me, but special classes were organised by the Jewish Committee. We had no books, no schoolbooks, nothing. As I was always the one to write very fast, I wrote word by word what the teacher was saying, and that was the textbook which the whole class shared. I still have those notes...

Anna Blasiak: After the war you and your mother had to live under false names. The war has ended, but the antisemitism was still so bad that you couldn't really exist under your real names.

It was indeed very bad. When we moved back to Kraków in 1945, people were renting rooms out. We stayed with one such family. If only you could hear their conversations… "Bloody Jews! Jews this, Jews that." If they ever found out that we were Jewish… It was very bad, both in Lvov and in Kraków. I remember these few days in Lvov, when the city was completely free of the Germans and the Russians were still on the other side of town. No Germans and no Russians in Lvov, a 'free city'. Suddenly I heard a commotion… It sounded like horse's hooves. And from afar, I saw a Russian soldier on horseback, riding in. It was eerie, it was absolutely eerie. Nobody dared to go out, even though there were no Germans in town anymore. The Soviet officer got off the horse and walked by slowly. Suddenly I heard a shot. I didn't know what it was, but found out later that a Jewish man was hiding inside, under the floorboards, and when he saw the Russian officer, he ran out. Apparently he started kissing the officer's boot. Some Ukrainian man came out and shot him on the spot.

You lost contact with Frau Wieth in Lemberg, when she left you at St. George's Cathedral. Did you try to find her?

Of course, people were constantly looking for other people after the war. Everybody was putting little scraps of paper here and there with information that they were looking for this or that person. That's how life was then. People were gathering at the Jewish Committee in Kraków, looking for survivors, for family, for friends.

I had a friend, a young girl like myself. My friend and her parents survived, they were a family unit! Many lonely people were coming and gathering at their place. Many didn't have that, many had no-one... I often came to visit too, and met a number of people there. My friend and I just sat there and listened to other people's conversations. The male visitors were usually doing bartering, they were going to eastern Germany or to Czechoslovakia. They were surely black marketeering. Black market was the norm then, there was nothing untoward in it. You had to survive. They would bring a pair of tights, for instance, or a pair of stockings, and exchange them for butter or some other 'luxury'. It was all about bartering and black marketeering. These men at my friend's place were discussing their deals, their travels, where they went, what they brought, what they were taking and where they were going, that sort of thing.

And then it occurred to me that, since they were travelling to Germany, maybe they could try to find Frau Wieth for me? But how to describe her? How would they know that it was her? I only had a tiny photograph of her, her passport photo. The one and only thing I had of hers was this tiny photograph. So occasionally I would say to one of the men, "Do you mind if I ask you a favour?" He was leaving the following morning. "I have a photograph here. Have a look." "What do you want me to do?" he asked. "Nothing, I just want you to memorise the face." And I described what she looked like. "Who knows, maybe you'll come across her somewhere. She has rather unique looks. She is very tall and stands very upright. She is noticeable. She is not one of many, she's one of a kind."

It went on for quite some time. This person was going, another one was going. And I was always telling them the same story, showing them the photo, describing what Frau Wieth looked like, what her hairstyle was like. She wouldn't change her hairstyle, she was very conservative. It was always the same. And she liked wearing white blouses and suits.

Nothing happened. And then one day I came home and my mother said, "Lili, you're going to London." "I'm going to London? What? What are you saying to me?" When I was a girl, my father always taught me things. I learned how to read and write at a very early age. He always said, "If you are a good pupil, if you are studious, I will send you to school in England. I will send you to London." But what did I know about London when I was five, six or even seven years of age? And suddenly now my mother said, "You're going to London!" "Well, what do you mean?" I wanted to know. "How so? How am I going to London?" She explained, "I just had some news. There is a rabbi from London who is collecting Jewish children and taking them to England. He's in Warsaw right now and he already has a list. You were put on this list without us knowing." "Am I to go to London without you?" I asked. "Yes, without me." "Well, then I'm not going." "No, you'll go, you'll go." And that was that! I was to leave within a week, it was all very short notice. This rabbi could only take so many children and somehow, miraculously to me, I was added to the list.

So the following day I told my friend, "You know, how amazing! I'm going to London." "Are you crazy?" I had to explain everything. "I can't believe it," she said. "Come home with me. Let's go and tell my parents. Maybe I could go too?" We went to hers and it was the usual thing: people coming and going. There was a visitor there, whom I saw there quite often, but this time he didn't even take his coat off. I remember him so vividly. He had a lovely coat, wasn't dressed shabbily at all. He said, "I haven't got much time. I only came to say goodbye, because I'm off tomorrow morning. I'm going to Germany." So they asked him what he was taking, what he was bringing back, all the usual stuff. And I said, "Oh, could you hold on just one moment? May I please have a piece of paper, somebody? And a pen? Will you wait a minute, Mr Kraus?" And I sat down. This was the first time I did that – I wrote a note in German: 'Dear Frau Wieth, I am leaving for London on such-and-such a date. I may not be able to contact you again, but if this note reaches you, please know that I'm alive, that we are both alive, my mother and I, and that I've gone to London. I'm leaving Poland on 22 March.' I put it in an envelope, put her name on it, and turned to the man, "Could you please take that?" I explained everything to him the usual way. I showed him the photograph and explained that she was very tall, taller even than him, and he was not a short man. And I gave him the letter. "If you ever come across a person matching this description, please approach her. It might just be her. This is my last chance. I shall never be able to do that when I am in London." He took the letter, said goodbye and left. That letter reached her...

How?

I've never seen him afterwards, I have never had a chance to thank him. I believe that he was going to Germany, to eastern Germany, via Czechoslovakia. They were doing black marketeering in the camps, bringing food and other things to the people there. He went inside one such camp. People were queuing for soup. It was lunchtime. He went about his business there and suddenly he saw a woman towering over everybody else. He came up to her and said, "Are you Frau Wieth?" She looked at him and said, "Yes, I am." "I have a letter for you." He handed the letter to her without another word and was gone. He simply gave her the letter and disappeared. Of all the times I tried, of all the people I sent out looking for her, it was *this one*, the one who came and said he was in such a hurry that he wouldn't even take his coat off...

She found you in London afterwards...

Being educated, as she was, speaking three languages fluently, including English, she immediately wrote to the main Aliens Department of the Home Office in Piccadilly, in Swallow Street. She knew exactly what to do, where to send the letter. She wrote in the letter that there was a girl by the name of so-and-so who should have arrived in London around the end of March, because she left Poland on 22 March, and that she was looking for her. And she gave her address.

I was at my London school at the time and suddenly I

was called to the headmaster's office. I thought, "What have I done now? My god! I am called to the headmaster's!" We all feared him. He carried a stick and was a terribly strict man. So I came into his office and here was a police officer! The headmaster said, "Lili, you're going to go with this officer now." Not a word of explanation. I thought I was being deported! "Why is the policeman taking me away? I'm at school, I haven't done anything and I came here officially!" All that was going through my head. I went with this officer who didn't say one word to me on our journey in the police car, not a word. Not that I could say much in English either, because it was just a few weeks after I arrived in England. My English was practically non-existent. I could just about communicate on a very basic level.

He brought me to the police station, took me upstairs and knocked at the door. There was a huge room and a big desk, behind which another police officer was sitting. "Come in, sit down." There was a chair in front of his desk. I sat down. And then he started asking me all sorts of questions. "Why did you come here? How did you come here? Who have you got here? Where? Why are you here on your own?" Of course he knew *everything* about me, but he still asked all those questions! It was like in the films. I was trying to answer his questions, struggling with the language, and I was, of course, very frightened. I didn't know what they wanted from me. I really thought I was being deported.

Suddenly I laid my eyes on an envelope and a letter on his desk. Frau Wieth's handwriting was as large and tall, as she was. She wrote in Gothic, in big letters, which were not leaning to the right, like for most of us, but to the left. When

I saw the letter, I exclaimed, "Frau Wieth!" And the man said, "Indeed, Frau Wieth. Who *is* Frau Wieth?" It got really very unpleasant, because there she was, a German woman, sending a letter to me, barely in this country since March... I have no idea what she wrote in it. He never gave me the letter. And it wasn't two or three lines, it was quite a long letter. What did she tell them? The man knew about everything, he knew it all, yet he still asked me all those questions! And I said, "She saved my life during the war." "Huh? A German woman saved your life?! How is that?" "Well, she did," I said. "She saved mine and my mother's life during the war." "Tell me about it." So I told him, "She is a German and she kept us in hiding." He was adamant. He couldn't fathom that a German person could have *saved* me. He said, "How come? You're Jewish. Aren't you Jewish?" "Yes, I'm Jewish." "So how come a German person saved your life?" It was very difficult for him to comprehend. He only heard of the atrocities. He didn't hear of any cases like mine. I did my best to explain. "Well, really? Amazing... But all right, that's fine, you can go now." And that was that.

That's how I found her and how she found me!

The police officer kept the letter. How I wish I had it...

Who was Rabbi Solomon Schonfeld, thanks to whom you found your way to England?

He was such a gorgeous man! You can't imagine what he looked like. He was six feet two and had the looks of a film star. And the presence of this man, his charisma... He called himself 'One of God's Cossacks'. Achieving his aim was all that mattered. And the idea was to get the surviving Jewish children out of Poland and bring them to England, by hook or by crook. He managed to do it, because nobody could withstand his power of persuasion. He was so charismatic and so absolutely stunning in that uniform of his! You would never say that this was an Ultra Orthodox rabbi. He looked like an aristocratic English officer. The uniform was made up, it wasn't real. He invented it, because he realised that Poles have a penchant for a military uniform. If he went there in his normal attire, looking like a rabbi, he knew he might not achieve much. But when he walked in, dressed as an English officer, every official stood to attention. In that uniform, there wasn't a thing he couldn't do. He was a maverick. He certainly was one in a million!

Doctor Rabbi Solomon Schonfeld

He travelled with us, children, on the Swedish boat called SS Ragne. I stayed very close to him, because I was translating for him and the children, I was the go-between. The children spoke no English and he knew no Polish. I spoke German, as did he, and that was how we communicated. He taught us songs, wonderful, funny, very English songs, also patriotic songs, like 'Rule Britannia' or 'Tipperary', not to mention the national anthem. He explained things to us about England. He wanted to incite the interest in the country the children were going to, so was telling us about it, teaching us popular English songs. All to keep the children together, and interested. He was marvellous, we all adored him! What a mind! He remembered everything about every child, where he or she came from, what he or she did, what his and her parents did. He knew everything about each child he brought to England, and he brought over close to four thousand of them...

First I travelled from Kraków to Gdynia by train and then on the boat from Gdynia. The journey took seven days, we arrived in England on my birthday! What a birthday present! On approach to Tilbury, the Tower Bridge opened for us. What a sight that was! I have photographs of the boat under the bridge. There was a barrage of photographers on the quay in Tilbury, photographers and journalist awaiting us. Ours was the first out of three transports from Poland. Just before the outbreak of war, Doctor Schonfeld brought children from other countries, from Hungary and Czechoslovakia, but this was the first one he organised after the war. It was March 1946.

Doctor Schonfeld's father had built several Jewish schools in England, and Rabbi Schonfeld became their president. We had professors and teachers who were Oxford dons. These were religious schools, outstanding educationally! They still are. When you look at the list of Oxbridge students and you check which schools they went to, Doctor Schonfeld's schools are very high on the list. Doctor Schonfeld sent me to one of his excellent schools immediately. In those days there were mostly boys there, but there were also a few girls. Nowadays there is a separate girls' school and a separate boys' school. I found myself in a totally alien environment, I was not brought up in Orthodoxy, but here I had to comply, even though I wasn't very happy about it. I was treated very well though. There were a few of us from the transport and we were seen as something rather exotic.... But the masters were very understanding and interested in us. I learned the language reasonably quickly and could confer with the teachers, I could answer their questions. One of the masters, who was from Germany, loved the fact that I spoke German. As a result I had quite a few privileges in the boarding house, because he was the House Master. He would allow me to go out, when others couldn't. For instance, I could go to Polish-Jewish Ex-Combatants Association Club situated in Stamford Hill and be with my people. I usually came back a little later than I should, but he allowed that. On top of that we did quite a lot of singing together, and I loved to sing. He had a very good voice. One of the other masters accompanied him on the piano and he sang arias from operas. One day he said, "Lili, I'm going to ask you to come down in the evening." And we had to be in bed by eight o'clock. "You'll come down to the

171

Masters' Room and we're going to sing duets." It was wonderful! He was the first one to teach me some opera duets. We sang from Mozart, we sang from Rossini. I loved that! He was very outgoing and kind to me, though otherwise very strict and rather 'Germanic' in his behaviour. The children were quite frightened of him, but that didn't worry me. He was always very nice to me.

Did you talk about your wartime experiences with other friends at school or teachers? Or was it something that you didn't want to talk about?

Not with the children, not with school colleagues or friends. They wouldn't understand. But their parents were very interested and they often invited me over. That was before my mother came. They would invite me on a Sunday, 'for tea'. They wanted to know things, wanted to hear things. They were a great help in bringing my mother to England.

It was more than a year before your mother came over. It must have been very hard for you. It was the first time ever that you were properly apart.

It was hard, because I knew she was there on her own. That was the hardship. While I had it good, I had everything, I was well looked after, I had food to eat, clothes to wear and school to study at, she was there, struggling. Everything was fine, but I worried terribly about my mother being there, in Poland, on her own.

Were you in regular contact?

We wrote letters. I was at a boarding school then. We boarded not where the actual school was, the boarding house was in Hampstead Heath, the school in Hendon. My underground station was Hampstead. It was on top of the Heath. It was a fabulous place, we were right on top of the hill, with the whole of London spreading underneath.

How did you manage to bring your mother over?

I was desperate to be reunited with her. I asked whoever and wherever I could, to help me. Rabbi Schonfeld kept trying, the school and some of my schoolmates' parents tried too. In the end it was the school secretary, Mr. Katzenberg and his wife, as well as Doctor Schonfeld, who succeeded! The idea was to bring her over as a domestic for the school, because there was a shortage of English staff, cleaners, cooks. So that was how they managed to get her a permit. It wasn't easy. She got a permit as 'a domestic', and arrived in May 1947...

You were, however, not allowed to go and meet her at the station...

That was because she arrived on a Shabbat, on Saturday. I wasn't allowed to go to the station. "What do you mean?" I said. "My mother is coming and I'm not going to meet her?" They locked me in and I couldn't get out.

My mother arrived with one suitcase, five pounds in

her pocket, and a sewing machine. We had a kind of spiritual father in Poland, a man who was also in hiding thanks to Metropolitan Sheptytsky. His name was Rabbi Doctor Kahane. After I had left for England, my mother spent a great deal of time with his family, as their guest. It was he who arranged everything for her, just like a year before he arranged for me to be put on the 'Schonfeld's list'. And he told her, "You're going to a totally strange, new land, with a new language, new everything. What are you going to do? How are you going to support yourself? You have a profession. You can make things, you can do wonders with your hands, but that's not enough. You need to have a tool. You've got to take the machine." And he somehow managed to get a permit for her to bring her sewing machine with her.

Lili Stern with her mother Cecylia Stern, London 1947

So there she was, at the station, with the suitcase, the sewing machine and five pounds in her pocket. And nobody there to meet her! She didn't speak English. She could understand a little bit, but that was all. I remember they had some English lessons before the war at home, my father, my mother and some of their friends. My father was a great Anglophile before the war. As a result, my mother could understand a bit of English, but couldn't speak any. She stood there at the station and waited, and waited, and waited. And nobody came. Eventually one of the porters came up to her and asked if he could help her. She said, "School," and gave him the address. "All right, I'll put you in a taxi and tell the driver to take you there."

It was a terrible experience for me. The way I was brought up was that if somebody's going away, we put them on the train or on the bus. If somebody is arriving, we meet them at the station. It was always like that. And suddenly she arrived in a strange country and nobody was there to meet her! I was in a real state. I said that I wanted to speak to Doctor Schonfeld. "What sort of hypocrisy is this? You don't allow me to go and welcome my mother in a foreign land because of Shabbat, but she is allowed to come to school by taxi? Tell me, is that right? Is that what the religion dictates?"

Doctor Schonfeld didn't have it easy with me, oh, no. I rebelled about a number of things. Every single morning we had to get up at six o'clock for prayers, and afterwards we had breakfast and were taken to school, as it was on different premises. The prayers were in Hebrew, you read the Bible in Hebrew. At first I was reading it, like everybody else, without really understanding, but after a while I realised what exactly I was reading. I realised that it said in Hebrew, 'Thank you, dear Lord, for having created me a man.' Before, I was just repeating it like a parrot, I was repeating things without having any idea what they meant, but when I understood what I was saying, I walked out.

Doctor Schonfeld asked me about it and I told him, "I am not a man. I'm a girl. A woman. Why should I get up at six o'clock in the morning to pray and thank the Lord for being a man? No!" He knew me and he knew that to win this one, would not be easy, so all he said was "Lili, please, behave." I didn't go to the prayers anymore.

So your mother finally arrived at the school. Was she then staying where you were?

For a while, yes. It was wonderful. From then on we didn't need to worry about anything. My mother, being my mother, would design and make anything out of nothing, so she immediately had ladies interested in her skills. She started working almost straightaway. She had what they called 'golden hands'. She was not a burden on anyone.

When my mother was here, we both started looking for a way to bring Frau Wieth over as well. Of course it was difficult, with her being German, but we had people who wanted to help us. Many people in London were interested in us, because we had survived the war 'over there'. They hadn't met any survivors before us. At my school the children, having no idea, looked at us as if we weren't from the same planet! It wasn't easy, but my mother soon made very good friends. There were social gatherings on Sundays, where we had an opportunity to interest others in helping us to bring Frau Wieth over. It was the same idea again, to bring her over as a domestic, as a working force. That's how we managed to get her to England in the end.

It was marvellous to have her with us, but Frau Wieth, being a proud person, didn't want to be a burden, so was desperate to find a job. We started looking for people needing a housekeeper or a governess. Somebody recommended her to their friends, but she was very unhappy there. They treated her abominably.

She never ever told anyone about what she did during the war. She just didn't talk about it. So nobody knew, unless they knew it from us. I would sometimes inadvertently splurge something, not knowing that she didn't tell them. The people she worked for didn't know. And she suffered for being German.

Eventually she said, "This is not good, something needs to be done. I'll go to America. Things may be different there." And somehow we managed to pull it off, we managed to arrange it. How could you get to America then? It wasn't just a question of buying a ticket and flying. It was very difficult, but she registered with the American Embassy and went through the whole process. It took about two years or so, but eventually she was allowed to go. And she went. It so happened that later I was also in America, so we were there together. She worked for a Jewish family and she was very, very happy there. She loved the people she was working for. When, after ten years in the States, I came back to England with my daughter Karen, Frau Wieth used to visit us on holidays. When the people she worked for died, she came back here to England for good. She had always wanted to live in England. At first she stayed with me and then she moved to the coast. She wanted to be by the sea, so we moved her to Worthing. She died in 1981.

She was like a beloved family member. My mother, my Karen and I were the closest thing to any family she had. She loved me. And she loved my Karen. She thought nobody in the whole world was like us; that Karen and I, we were unique. She never uttered a word of German after the war, not one word of German, ever. When exchanging letters with my mother, my mother always wrote to her in German and Frau Wieth always answered in English.

Your mother came in 1947. Two years later you managed to bring Frau Wieth over. You were 19 then and you were a student ...

I studied languages and commercial studies. I spoke quite a few languages. I liked languages. I spoke Polish, Russian, Ukrainian, German, English, Spanish, Italian and French. I belonged to the Linguist Club in London and did some courses there too, on top of studies. I wanted to become a simultaneous interpreter. I thought it was my calling, but I couldn't do it. It was simply too difficult and occasionally my nerves gave way. It was such a stress. I even tried for the BBC to do simultaneous interpreting on the news, but it was too much. I did stenotyping and would have wanted to be an interpreter at international conferences. Eventually I gave that dream up. But I did become a translator, occasionally an interpreter.

I never learnt Yiddish. I didn't even know about the district of Kazimierz[26] in Kraków before the war. I was never there. We lived in the centre of Kraków, in the so-called 'old town', and I had no need to go to Kazimierz. My mother went occasionally on a Friday night to listen to the great Rabbi Ozjasz Thon. He was an orator and people, even non-Jews, would fill Tempel synagogue to listen to him. My mother went there on Fridays, but I never knew where she went. Today when I see Kazimierz, it's become more like Montmartre. I find it very painful. I don't find it fun. It's like dancing on the graves of those who lived there before the war and perished in the Holocaust...

When we started coming to Kraków with my husband Peter and visited the area for the first time, it was during the Festival of Jewish Culture. We were in a restaurant and I stood by the window on the first floor and looked outside. There were people dancing to enormously loud music coming from the stage. People were enjoying themselves. And on the opposite side there was an old, empty house with black windows, like hollow eye sockets. It was all too painful to behold...

We lived a so-called 'normal life', but when I saw that... It's not that I stood there crying, because I didn't. I might even have been singing along. But it was, oh, so painful to see such enjoyment and people dancing on a 'street of graves', more a cemetery than a street...

---

[26] Kazimierz is a historical district of Kraków, for many centuries a place of coexistence and interpenetration of ethnic Polish and Jewish cultures. The Jewish inhabitants of the district were forcibly relocated in 1941 by the German occupying forces into the Kraków ghetto just across the river in Podgórze. Today Kazimierz is one of the major tourist attractions of Krakow and an important centre of cultural life of the city.

I visit schools in this country every now and then, to tell my story and the story of the Extraordinary Ordinary People, who helped others to survive the cataclysm of the war. Some time ago I was asked to present awards to children to whom I had spoken before. And these children asked to see me again. They wanted me to come again and present them with the award they were getting. Of course I couldn't say no. There I was, two hours each way, going to Barking. When I arrived, ten children were sitting there, around the table, waiting for me. They were all about the age I was at the time when I escaped from the ghetto, 11 or 12. The headmaster greeted me and said to the children, "Look, if you would like to ask Lili a question, I'm sure she won't mind answering. So don't be shy. You can speak if you want to say something." A boy came forward. I asked him what his name was "My name is Samir." "Okay, Samir, what would you like to say?" "Remember, you told us that you were lying in the snow when you escaped from the ghetto?" he said. The boy, I believe, was Muslim, he was 11. "How long did you lie in the snow?" he asked. "I can't tell you," I said. "I don't know. I didn't have a watch and even if I had, I don't think I would have looked. I can't say." I was astounded that he remembered such a detail. This question clearly bothered him. How long can one lie in the snow and not freeze to death, then get up and go? Just imagine. Then a little girl came forward, "You said you were hidden by this German lady. Did you *trust* her?" What a question from a girl of 11 or 12! One young Muslim girl was so moved by my little brother Uriel – who perished, aged six-and-a-half, in Bełżec – that she remembered him on a stone, which says, "Uriel Stern, 1935-1942. You have always been loved and will never be forgotten.

From your sister, Lili'. The original stone is now at the Jewish Cemetery at Miodowa Street in Kraków, and a replica of the stone is at the Jewish Cemetery in Hoop Lane in London.

Stone commemorating Lili's brother, Uriel Stern

When I am confronted with such moments, I realise how important it is to talk about it, particularly to children. Sometimes, I think, "Who cares? Who is interested to listen or read about it?" But then I think about these children, how attentively they listened to what I had to say. I think about the questions they asked... They are amazing. And what their good teachers do is amazing! These are extraordinary teachers. It's thanks to them that these children will learn how to grow up into decent human beings. The more I speak to these youngsters of today, the more I feel that there is hope for this world of ours, after all...

Lili with a group of children

Historical Context
July 1945 – 1952
Clare Mulley

Stalin secured Soviet influence across Eastern Europe at the Potsdam Conference in the summer of 1945. Poland's Jewish communities had been all but completely erased, much of the country lay in ruins, and the remaining resistance was now systematically rooted out. In effect a Soviet satellite, post-war Poland's borders were renegotiated and its government-in-exile was replaced by a Soviet-backed Communist regime.

Lili was in Kraków when the two nuclear bombs at Hiroshima and Nagasaki brought the Second World War to an end. The Japanese surrender was signed on 2 September 1945. She reached London the following March. While Britain and most of Europe began rebuilding after post-war elections, the Soviet-managed elections in Poland in 1947 delivered a state socialist system. Five years later, in July 1952, the country officially became the People's Republic of Poland. The political thaw would not start until after Stalin's death the following year.

Clare Mulley, 24 September 2020
www.claremulley.com

CHAPTER SIX
LATER LIFE
After 1952

Lili with her daughter, Karen and her mother, Cecylia

After finishing school and her studies, Lili Stern went to Israel with an international Jewish students' organisation to learn contemporary Hebrew and work in a kibbutz. She was supposed to stay and work there for six weeks, but in the end she stayed for six months. She travelled around the country and had a chance to meet her father's elder brother, who had emigrated there as a young man. She also met the man who was to become her first husband. His name was Tolek Angstreich-Cadmon and he was also from Lwów. He was an officer in the Israeli army at the time, but Lili refused to be 'an army wife' and insisted on going back to London. She was soon followed by Tolek, who went on to study there. The couple were married in London by Rabbi Doctor Schonfeld in 1953. The following year Lili's mother, Cecylia, known as Cesia or Mimi, married Karol Abraham. That same year the Cadmons moved to the States. They lived in New York. That's where their daughter Karen was born.

Lili with her first husband, Tolek Cadmon

Lili worked at Broad Street and then, when Karen was about four years of age, as the PA to the Monaco Observer at the United Nations. She worked there during the 1960 Krushchev's shoe banging incident[27] and the Cuban Missile Crisis in 1962[28]. Being fluent in French, she was their

---

[27] Nikita Khrushchev's shoe-banging incident occurred during the 902nd Plenary Meeting of the United Nations General Assembly held in New York City in 1960. During the session on 12 October, Nikita Khrushchev, First Secretary of the Communist Party of the Soviet Union, pounded his shoe on his delegate-desk in protest at a speech by Philippine delegate Lorenzo Sumulong.

[28] The Cuban Missile Crisis, also known as the October Crisis of 1962, the Caribbean Crisis, or the Missile Scare, was a 13-day (16-28 October 1962) confrontation between the United States and the Soviet Union initiated by the American discovery of Soviet ballistic missile deployment in Cuba. The confrontation is often considered the closest the Cold War came to escalating into a full-scale nuclear war.

translator, and also ran their travel agency.

In 1963, after the Cadmons divorced, Lili and Karen returned to London. Karen was schooled in London at St Paul's girls' school, and then at Godolphin and Latymer, but eventually went back to America, where she married, had three children, and one grandchild. They all live in Florida.

Lili tied the knot again in 1975, to a well-known stage, film and television actor, Eric Pohlmann. They travelled extensively together on Eric's theatrical, TV and film engagements abroad. He died very suddenly in 1979, while the couple were in Salzburg for a festival, in which he was to appear, holding his always-present cigarette in one hand and a cup of coffee in the other.

Lili with her second husband, Eric Pohlmann

Lili's third husband was Peter Janson-Smith, whom she met in 1985. He was a well-known literary agent and copyright expert, a 'Prince among Agents', as Ian Fleming, whom he represented, called him. He also represented Kingsley Amis, John Gardner, Eric Ambler, Anthony Burgess and many other authors. Lili and Peter spent 31 happy years together, visiting their much-loved city of Kraków several times a year, and for many occasions. In the year 2012, the President of Kraków awarded Peter with the medal Honoris Gratia. Lili received the same honour in 2018.

Peter died in London in 2016.

Lili with her third husband, Peter Janson-Smith

Lili was very involved in Polish cultural life in London and became an unofficial 'ambassador' of Polish culture and art. She also put a lot of effort into the building of Polish-Jewish relations and was engaged in initiatives in London and elsewhere promoting them. It was she who first spread the word in London about Irena Sendler, a Catholic Polish woman responsible – together with others working with her – for rescuing hundreds and hundreds of Jewish children by smuggling them out of the Warsaw ghetto. Lili spoke about Mrs. Sendler in the British and European Parliaments. She was also involved in preserving the memory of Doctor Janusz Korczak (Henryk Goldszmit), Polish-Jewish pedagogue and author, who died in Treblinka together with nearly two-hundred orphans in his charge, despite being offered sanctuary by his Polish friends. Lili helped fundraise for two Korczak's memorials in Warsaw.

In 2007, for her extraordinary and distinguished services, Lili Pohlmann received one of Poland's highest accolades, the Knight's Cross of the Order of Merit of the Republic of Poland. She has also received a medal entitled "For People Doing Good", especially close to her heart. It was awarded to her by members of the International Irena Sendler Schools Association at their conference in Warsaw in 2013. Lili has been made an MBE in the Queen's Birthday Honours List 2020.

Lili lives in London in a beautiful, sunny apartment filled with books, paintings, music and photos of her dearest ones. And, of course, with memories.

Out of about 300 relatives on both her mother's and her father's side, only she and her mother Cecylia survived the war.

Lili and her mother, Cecylia, London 1986

AFTERWORD

By Aleksander B. Skotnicki

Lili Stern-Pohlmann is a multifaceted persona and very much deserves a closer look.

Her long and interesting life covers the pre-war period (i.e. her early childhood in Kraków), time spent in Lvov/Lemberg during the Second World War and immediately after the war, as well as the post-war period. These last 75 years were mainly spent in London, but they also include nearly ten years in New York, and numerous travels, and longer or shorter visits to Israel, Austria, Germany, France, as well as to Kraków and Warsaw. Through the prism of her story we can therefore explore times and places where she has been, where she grew up as a child and teenager, where she fought for survival in Lemberg, and finally where she lived life to the full, active and focused on building relations with people around her, to whom she was devoted and dear.

But first and foremost it is important to focus on Lili because of her rich personality, energy and deep passion, her dedication to reaching the goals, which she set for herself. She wanted to preserve the grateful memory of those who helped her, but also to promote the good in people's actions, to advance the development of the arts (especially of poetry, theatre and music) and finally to build a better world based on tolerance, interest and understanding of various cultural, national and religious groups.

Lili Pohlmann's achievements in building a better present and future are huge and not easy to comprehend. She met so many people throughout her life, she was involved in so many initiatives focused on the betterment of human relations, including between nations and religions, she inspired so many undertakings to commemorate people such as Janusz Korczak or Irena Sendler. All of this meant that she was and is one of the most recognisable people among the Polish exile community in London after the war.

I met Lili Pohlmann a dozen or so years ago, during one of her frequent visits to Kraków. I also visited her in London, in her welcoming home in Fitzjames Avenue. I always had a lot of respect for her love for Kraków, which she instilled into her husband, Peter, who used to celebrate his birthdays in Lili's childhood home-town. When in Kraków, she visited her friends; and they, too, paid her visits at the Hotel Francuski, where she always stayed. She is a member of the board of the Judaica Foundation, Center for Jewish Culture at 17 Meisels Street. She visited historical and art exhibitions which I organised, both in the gallery of the Stradom Dialogue Centre and at the Art Palace at Szczepański Square. She remains in regular contact with her friends based in Kraków and Warsaw – over the phone and via letters. I myself was the recipient of tens of letters, photographs, newspaper cuttings, copies of invitations, which I carefully collected in several folders, and used while writing my book about Lili in Polish (*Lili Stern-Pohlmann. Kraków, Lwów, Londyn*; Kraków 2017).

A lesson I learnt from Lili Pohlmann was optimism. She also taught me how to believe in pursuing one's intended goals (Korczak's monuments in Warsaw, speeches at the Polish Embassy in London devoted, first and foremost, to

Irena Sendler, including the naming of English schools in London after the most famous of Polish 'Righteous Among the Nations'). I admire Lili's memory and her regard for people who helped her and her mother during the Second World War. She pushed for their recognition, both in Israel, and in Poland. Lili is one of those who move the proverbial heaven and earth to achieve her noble goals.

Lili used to say, "I'm a stranger to prejudice and intolerance. I am Polish, but not Polish-Jewish, as often I am referred to. My religion is my personal thing." Many times over the years she organised Christmas dinners for her Christian friends. And she still does it. She stresses that she never judges people on their skin colour, nationality or religion, but only on their human decency. She calls for people to talk, to explore history, to get to know the truth. Narrow-mindedness and hostility are born out of lack of knowledge and ignorance. As London journalist Robert Małolepszy wrote a while ago, "You can listen to Lili Pohlmann for hours. Looking at this cheerful lady, full of warmth and kindness, a sheer embodiment of tolerance and openness, it is difficult to believe that she went through hell."

She always says that there are no good and bad nations, races or religions. Only good and bad people. "My father and little brother were denounced by a Ukrainian and killed by Germans. My mother and I was saved by a German lady and by a Greek Catholic archbishop and Ukrainian nuns. Who am I to measure the good or the bad in each of those nations? All I know is that for the good to conquer evil, prejudice and stereotypes must be rooted out of our lives," she stresses. "Let me finish with a famous quote by Edmund Burke, 'The only thing necessary for the triumph of evil is for good men to do nothing.'"

Kraków
July 2020

ACKNOWLEDGEMENTS

By Anna Blasiak

First and foremost I would like to give my wholehearted thanks to Lili Pohlmann, for agreeing to share her story and for all the hours of conversations in her beautiful London flat, over tea and cake.

I would like to express my gratitude to Professor Aleksander Skotnicki, who first brought the story of Lili Pohlmann to my attention in his Polish book about her, and who was also always there to help me with the archival material. Professor Skotnicki kindly agreed to write the Afterword to this book.

I am very grateful to Philippe Sands QC, who shares Lili's origins in Lwów, for his kindness and for taking the time to write the warm and insightful Introduction to the book. My appreciation also to Clare Mulley who wrote astute historical commentaries throughout the book.

Special thanks to Antony Lishak for all his help and support, as well as to Lili's daughter, Karen Mantell.

Thank you to Robert Peett of Holland House Books for taking an interest in this story and for believing that it needed to be told; also for the help in shaping this book.

I would also like to acknowledge with gratitude the support of the Polish Cultural Institute in London, and especially of Director Robert Szaniawski (now in New York) and Magda Raczyńska, Head of Literature.

Without all of the above this book would not have happened.

Ramsgate
July 2020

Anna Blasiak is a poet, translator, journalist and literature co-ordinator of the European Literature Network. She has translated over 40 books of fiction, non-fiction as well as some poetry between Polish and English (also as Anna Hyde). In addition to her book-length translations, her work has been published in *Best European Fiction 2015*, *Asymptote*, *The Guardian*, *B O D Y Literature*, *ANMLY*, *Modern Poetry in Translation* and *York Literary Review*. Anna has a particular interest in the Holocaust stories (she is the translator of Irit Amiel and Renia Spiegel).

Anna writes poetry in Polish and in English. She has been shortlisted for several major poetry competitions in Poland. Her bilingual book *Kawiarnia przy St James's Wrena w porze lunchu / Café by Wren's St-James-in-the-Fields, Lunchtime* is out now.

Clare Mulley is an award-winning author and historian. Her first book, *The Woman Who Saved the Children*, won the Daily Mail Biographers' Club Prize, and *The Spy Who Loved* led to Clare being decorated with Poland's national honour, the Bene Merito. Clare's third book, *The Women Who Flew for Hitler*, tells the extraordinary story of two women at the heart of Nazi Germany, whose choices put them on opposite sides of history. Clare reviews non-fiction for the *Telegraph* and *Spectator*. A popular public speaker, she has given a TEDx talk at Stormont, spoken at the Houses of Parliament, Royal Albert Hall, Imperial War Museum, National Army Museum and British Library, as well as many festivals. Recent radio and TV includes series and commentaries for the BBC, ITV, Channel 4, Channel 5 and the History Channel.

Philippe Sands QC is Professor of Law at University College London and a practising barrister at Matrix Chambers. He is author of *East West Street: On the Origins of Crimes Against Humanity and Genocide* (2016), which won the 2016 Baillie Gifford Prize and other awards, and *The Ratline: Love, Lies and Justice on the Trail of a Nazi Fugitive* (2020), which is also available as a BBC podcast. Philippe is President of English PEN and a member of the Board of the Hay Festival.

Prof. Aleksander Bartłomiej Skotnicki (born 24 August 1948) is a Polish haematologist and bone marrow transplantologist, professor of medicine, Head of the Haematology Clinic of the Jagiellonian University Medical College between 1993–2018, academic lecturer, social activist and member of the Polish Academy of Sciences. He is the grandson of a teacher Anna Sokołowska who died in 1945 in KL Ravensbrück, where she had been sent for helping her former Jewish pupils, and who was recognised by Yad Vashem in 1989. Author of several publications devoted to Jewish society of the pre-war Kraków. Founder of the Dialogue Centre in Kraków and the photographic archive of Jewish families of Kraków. Researcher and great friend of Holocaust survivors saved by Oskar Schindler, Chiune Sugihara and Polish Righteous Among the Nations.

Photographic Credits:

Page 41 Szkoła Powszechna im. Scholastyki w Krakowie, Kraków 1937

Page 51 Imperial War Museum, London © IWM HU 55553

Page 65 National Digital Archive, Poland

Page 117 Instytut Pamięci Narodowej (Institute of National Remembrance), Poland

Page 139 Central State Archive in Lviv

All other photographs come from Lili Stern-Pohlmann's personal archive

"Lili Pohlmann is the most remarkable person I have ever met. Her story is at once a testament to humanity and a profound and timely warning of what can happen to us all when that humanity is denied by political leaders. It should be required reading in these troubled times. I am proud to call her a friend."

—James O'Brien, Broadcaster, LBC

"A moving and important book, a conversation between two immigrants who started their new lives in London. Lili, as one of the last remaining eyewitnesses of Shoah, reveals the story of her life to Anna, talks about her Jewish family, relays her memories, also the tragic ones and shares startling truths about war, at the same time giving us hope and a message for the future. Highly recommended."

—Wioletta Greg, author of *Swallowing Mercury* longlisted for the Man Booker International 2017 and *Finite Formulae & Theories of Chance* shortlisted for the Griffin Poetry Prize 2015

"It is a life story of an extraordinary person who lost her happy childhood and had to tread a path of suffering and pain, but has never lost hope, courage, dignity and ability to love and forgive, devoting her life to ensure that never again will evil prevail."

—Witold Sobków, former Polish Ambassador in the UK

I started reading Lili and couldn't put the book down! The story is narrated in such a captivating way. I read a great deal about the Holocaust, academic books as well as personal narratives, and find this book outstanding in many ways. Clearly Lili's personality is unique and bringing to life such a horrendous historical era using a variety of small facts — with almost no historical arguments — makes her story overwhelming. I found this book truly outstanding. And the interaction between Lillie and Anna Blasiak is fascinating.

—**Emanuela Barasch Rubinstein, author of** *Mephisto in the Third Reich, The Devil, the Saints, and the Church: Reading Hochhuth's The Deputy,* **and** *Five Selves.*

"Due to the extraordinary kindness of strangers during The Holocaust, as well as their own remarkable ingenuity, Lili Pohlmann and her mother were the only survivors of an extended family of over three hundred. This is the incredible story of how that happened, yet for Lili the more significant question has always been *why*. Why, when so many were cruelly taken, was she chosen to live? The relentless search for an answer to that unanswerable question has infused that life with purpose. Lili is the embodiment of empathy with a unique talent for bringing people together – witnessed by her successful career as a translator and interpreter. Her kindness and generosity has touched innumerable hearts of all ages, and her indomitable spirit has enriched countless lives. Lili's voice, so sensitively captured on these pages, brims with humanity; as you, dear reader, are about to see, time spent in her company is always a pleasure."

—**Antony Lishak, CEO Learning from the Righteous**